Leapreneur

How to Take the Leap from Employee to Entrepreneur

Jerry Ilao

Disclaimer

This book is intended for informational purposes only.

This book includes information, products, and services by third parties. The use of recommended Third Party Material does not guarantee success and/or earnings related to you or your business. Publication of such Third Party Material is simply a recommendation and an expression of the author's own opinion of that material.

Links to Third Party Resources may be affiliate links, meaning the author may receive compensation if a service is ultimately purchases from such a link.

No part of this publication shall be reproduced, transmitted, or sold in whole or in part in any form, without the prior written consent of the author. All trademarks and registered trademarks appearing in this book are the property of their respective owners.

Users of this guide are advised to do their own due diligence when it comes to making business decisions and all information, products, and services that have been provided should be independently verified by your own qualified professionals. By reading this guide, you agree that the author is not responsible for the success or failure of your business decisions relating to any information presented in this book.

Your FREE Bonus

As a small token of thanks for buying this book, I'd like to offer a free bonus gift, my **Entrepreneur I N S I G H T S**, exclusive to the readers of this book.

The *Entrepreneur INSIGHTS* is a condensed list of my TOP 8 learnings as entrepreneur. It took me 15 *years of hands-on experience* and reflection before I was able to lay down the key things you need to remember in starting a business.

I hope that with what you will learn from this book, together with my FREE Top 8 INSIGHTS, I will be able to guide you well towards your dream of becoming a successful entrepreneur.

You can download the free gift here:

http://www.leapreneur.com/FREE

Acknowledgements

I would like to dedicate this book to my loving wife, Rio, and to our children, Justin, Reese, and Rylie. You have been very supportive to me and have given me the reason to continue doing what I do.

Likewise, thank you very much to my parents, brothers, and sister, as well as to my parents-in-law and brother-in-law.

To the AFFI Board of Directors, secretariat, and members, thank you for continuously inspiring me to hone my entrepreneurial skills and to break new grounds. I am so fortunate to be with the AFFI Family.

Lastly, to Almighty God, I dedicate my knowledge for Your greater glory.

Table of Contents

My Humble Story

I was born in Naga City, Philippines, located about 377 kilometres southeast of Manila, to a humble family of 7. My mother was a teacher and my father was a government employee. If you'd ask me, I didn't really have any background in running a business while growing up.

In 1991, I set my first steps in Ateneo de Naga High School. It was a dream come true because I really wanted to be an Atenean, aside from the fact that my mother taught there for many years. In high school, I became active in sports (basketball) and in student government. No, I was not at the top of my class, but sometimes I would get a chance to qualify for the honor's list.

Then came my senior year; it was inevitable. I had to decide what to take in college. It was a simple decision for me; I just wanted to have money and a nice house. I looked to our neighbors who were well-off and asked what their occupations were. It turned out that most of them were bank managers. I went to my father and asked him, *"Pa (Dad), how can I become a bank manager?"* When he replied that I would have a competitive edge if I were a *Certified Public Accountant (CPA),* I decided that this would be it!

Something was different when I took Accountancy in Ateneo de Naga University in 1995. I said to myself that I would be a CPA and that I wouldn't settle for being just an ordinary student anymore. I knew that if I wanted to have a good life and be a bank manager someday, I would have to excel. I would have to know my craft inside out. At the same time, I also didn't want the boring home-school-home routine so I joined organizations. I became very active in our home organization, *Junior Philippine Institute of Accountants (JPIA)*.

When I was in 3rd year, one of my favorite teachers advised me against running for the JPIA presidency and told me to concentrate on my studies instead. He was worried that my extra-curricular activities would negatively affect my studies and eventually, I would have a hard time passing the board exam. But then, believing that I could do it, I pushed through with my plan of becoming the JPIA President.

I believe that's where I learned my first life-changing lesson: *"If I put my mind and effort into something, I can do it!"* From an ordinary student in High School, I graduated Valedictorian of my class. I also qualified for Magna Cum Laude, along with nabbing 7 other awards during graduation. Aside from these, I was chosen as one of the Ten Outstanding Students of the Philippines (TOSP) and the Most Outstanding JPIAn of the Philippines.

After graduating, I took the Accounting Board Exam. It was during this time that I was invited by a multinational consumer goods company, Procter & Gamble, to take their employment exam. It was an honor to even be considered because the company is known for its very stringent hiring standards. After a few weeks, I was called for an interview and before I knew it, I was hired by that company right after passing the board.

I entered the corporate world and then quickly realized how lucky I was to be in that company, not only in terms of financial rewards but also in terms of the training and the wealth of knowledge that I received. I handled different roles--from plant accounting, to sales finance, to Global Internal Audit, and later on, to a Global Anti-Fraud Team.

It was indeed a very fulfilling career. But deep inside, I already felt early on that something was missing. So while working for P&G, I also started to engage in various small-time business ventures funded with my savings because I felt a strong interest in entrepreneurship ever since.

First Salvo

My first venture in business was a boutique in 2001. Yes, you read it right, a *boutique*... from a **straight man** (Sorry, I had to emphasize it to avoid any doubts)! During weekends, I would go to the busy streets of *Divisoria* market to buy my merchandise of ladies' shirts, blouses, etc. Despite the crowded place and the *"not-so-good"* smell around the area, I kept searching for quality yet classy designs at affordable prices. After I bought them, the clothes were sent to the shipping company who delivered them to my hometown, Naga City.

My parents were very supportive and greatly helped with running the business since they handled everything else, like retrieving the merchandise from the shipping company's warehouse, bringing them to my small shop in downtown Naga, displaying them for sale, selling them to customers, accounting the sales made and depositing them to my bank account.

For the first few months, the business was doing OK until I realized that the stocks were getting harder to manage. We were carrying more designs and items than ever before, which made inventory management a nightmare. When purchasing stocks, I could only guess which designs would sell but the moment of truth would come when the customers saw the actual clothes.

When vendors from Metro Manila also came to the city to sell the same wares, our sales suffered and the inventory of unsold stocks kept increasing, especially when new designs came in. After almost a year of operation, I could not support it anymore so I closed it.

Lessons Learned:
1.) Managing many inventory items is hard. Determining which designs will sell and how much to order for each item can be really overwhelming.
2.) I have to take into account unsold inventory as designs are changing fast.
3.) Pricing the product at 2x the cost is not enough to cover unsold inventory, salaries of people, and rental for the store.

Second Round

My goal of becoming an entrepreneur was not shaken by my first business failure. After my first business venture failed within just a year of operation, I was ready to pursue another business in 2003.

I noticed that the mobile carwash business was becoming popular in Metro Manila so I decided to bring it to Naga City. This time around, it didn't have the same inventory management problems like in my first business. It was a service business and the first-of-its-kind in our province so it seemed like a good business opportunity for me.

I went into the *Mobile Carwash Business* with little understanding as to how the business really worked and what problems I could potentially encounter. For me, I believed the business was that simple. I thought it was a good idea since at that time, no one was offering a carwash in malls while the customers were shopping. Personally, I hate waiting and doing nothing for an hour while my car is being washed. Offering a carwash in the mall while customers do their shopping is then not only convenient for the customers but also, very easy to manage.

What I did not anticipate was the headache of actually operating the business. It was my first time to have real employees! Well, during my first venture, my parents were managing the business for me. When I hired my first six employees, I got a taste of what a business operation is truly like. I tried to make things simpler and easier to follow (since they did not finish college) and treated them the best way I knew how.

Unfortunately, I wasn't able to avoid employee-related problems. They were absent when you needed them, did sub-standard work, hardly looked for customers when I'm not around, disregarded work policies, and even committed theft. In short, I was shocked by the operation nightmare.

To make matters worse, I was *"managing"* the business long distance. I was working in Manila while my business was in Naga so it was extra difficult. Had I learned about it in advance, I could have prepared myself better but no one was there to guide me.

Lessons Learned:
1.) When you have a service-oriented business, the complexity of managing people is multiplied by the number of people you have. You have to deal with absenteeism, *"emotional sentiments, "favoritism,"* and make sure that everyone is motivated to do their job.
2.) Standardization of work is very important in a service business. Since I have 5 carwash staff members at that time, I had to train them well and make sure that their cleaning is according to our standards.
3.) It's good that I didn't have inventory in the carwash business. But it posed another problem, and that is accounting for sales. Since there is no "real" inventory to match with the sales, if a dishonest employee did not report the sales properly, it will be harder to spot compared to those with real inventory.

Third Round

Coming out of the mobile carwash business heavily bruised but not beaten, I then developed a small area in a mountain near our city. It started as a small place that I bought for my parents so they can have a place to rest, away from the hustle and bustle of city-life. My father liked to plant trees and vegetables so I thought that place would re-energize him, with its clean air and view overlooking our city (just like Tagaytay and Antipolo).

We then developed and landscaped the place to make it a simple but beautiful vacation area. A few weeks after, a friend visited and liked the place very much. He suggested that we convert it to a weekend grill restaurant so more people could relax there, especially because it had a stunning view of the city.

Being the aspiring entrepreneur that I was, I got excited about the idea of having a restaurant. We setup a simple menu and advertised on the radio that a view like Tagaytay overlooking the city was available in our restaurant.

It quickly created a buzz in the city and soon a lot of people came to our restaurant. However, after a few months of operating it and much to our dismay, we decided to abandon the place due to security concerns. It was another investment down the drain.

This time, I was really hurt. I was beginning to think that entrepreneurship may not be for me. At this point, I already **lost around P1M** trying different business! P1M of hard-earned money that I could have used to buy a new car!

The Knockout

In 2005, I found an interesting product that could save up to *96% on printer ink expenses*. This new technology had just come out in the market and compared to ink refills which could only give savings of up to 50% from the original cartridges; this Ink All-You-Can System could give up to 96% savings without suffering print quality.

I know for a fact that original cartridges can cost as much as buying a new printer. So if this product is any good, it would mean huge savings for students and companies who spend thousands of pesos buying original printer cartridges.

Learning from my previous businesses, it seemed to be a better opportunity for me. It did not have the huge inventory like my first business. It was also a combination of both product and service, so I get the best of both worlds. Lastly, it was a technology business which I had a very keen interest on. It felt that the stars were finally aligning to make my dream come true.

So I did intensive research about this product and studied how it worked. I had so many questions in mind, learning from my previous business attempts, so I spent most of my nights and weekends finding the right answers. I looked for companies selling them here in the Philippines and found only one, which started just a few months ago. I said to myself, *"This is it!"*

I got very excited and called up my mom to tell her about my new business. After I told her about it, she told me something I will never forget... *"Baka naman malugi ka ulit dyan. Magkano na naman kaya mawawala sayong pera? (How much money will you lose again this time?)"* I could sense the concern and worry in her voice because I already lost P1M trying to be an entrepreneur.

I knew I had to be strong and continue to believe in my passion so I simply told her, *"Ma, pasasaan ba't tatamaan ko rin yan! (Mom, I know someday I will hit it right!)"* Ink All-You-Can was then born.

I started Ink All-You-Can as a home business with P10,000 capitalization, a far cry from the P1M that I spent on my first 3 businesses. At first, I was doing everything from sales, delivery, installation, to customer service.

Since the product was really good, the overwhelming response from customers triggered the business to grow faster than expected. In a limited span of time, more and more customers who tried the product became "product ambassadors", especially when they experienced first-hand that the product really delivered what it promised -- good quality inks at more affordable prices. At last, consumers could now enjoy freedom from expensive original cartridges.

In January 2007, after working for 7 years and operating Ink All-You-Can for more than a year as a side business, I quit my job and went full-time with Ink All-You-Can. Soon, the company expanded to SM Supermalls including branches in SM Megamall, SM City San Lazaro, SM City Fairview, SM City North Edsa, and SM Mall of Asia, among others.

In 2012, I co-founded a start-up company with my wife, Rio, to focus on developing world-class business solutions for SMEs. I am privileged to have combined my experience as an owner of brick and mortar stores with my experience as a co-founder of a tech start-up, to bring unique insights and solutions to SMEs throughout the Philippines.

Today, Ink All-You-Can has close to 20 branches all over the Philippines, employing over a hundred people. It continues to be the force to reckon with in the alternative printer ink consumables industry. Our start-up company, on the other hand, is preparing to offer our business solutions to international clients this year.

Why I Wrote This Book

Last Christmas, I met an old friend who I had not seen for more than a decade. I was eager to catch up with him and hear his stories. He is now married to an officemate and has 2 little kids already. He was also very excited to share that he was promoted to a manager position and now handles a 10-person team. It seemed like he was enjoying his work.

After hearing his exciting stories, he asked me whether I was still with my first company. I said *"Ah, not anymore. I now manage my own small business."*

Upon hearing it, his face lit up and asked me more questions like *"How did you do it?" "Is it worth it?" "How do I know if my idea is worth pursuing?"* His questions kept coming one after another. As it turned out, he was contemplating on quitting his job. He wanted to start his own business because he felt that his job was taking too much time away from his family. He felt that when he got promoted, his salary increased along with the pressure and the responsibilities.

He compared climbing the corporate ladder to pushing a big rock to the top of a mountain. Initially, when you begin your career, it is manageable because the slope is *"pretty flat."* But as you go up, the slope becomes steeper so it's much harder to push the rock upwards. The higher you are in that corporate mountain, the *more difficult and harder it gets to have a simpler and happier life...* So he wanted a way out.

I was surprised to hear that from my friend. But on second thought, I remembered that I heard a lot of similar stories from other people as well: employees who were tired of their corporate jobs, employees who just dragged their feet every morning to go to work and employees who hated waking up so early and working late nights because they rarely see their children anymore.

Sadly, they felt that they were just *"living to work"* and couldn't do anything about it. They wanted a way out but they didn't know how. They were afraid because nobody was there to guide them. They read different books about starting a business, but they were all too generic and hard to apply. They couldn't find helpful resources to guide them with effectively transitioning from being an employee to an entrepreneur.

Every time I would hear such stories, the memories of me in those same shoes kept flashing in my mind. It was the time when I was also feeling tired with my job and I wanted more freedom and flexibility. Though I earned a sizable salary, my job was wearing me down and my eagerness to escape the corporate world grew each day that passed.

Good for me, I had the courage to start my own business, even when no one was there to guide me. I had my share of losses and failures but eventually, I made it! And now that I know better, I feel the responsibility to share what I know so that aspiring entrepreneurs can avoid the same mistakes that I made years ago. People always ask me, *"How did you do it?" "Can you give us tips?" "What do you think about this idea?" "How did you get your first customers?"*

Thus, I took it upon myself to write a book to share my story to everyone, to share my failures and successes, and most importantly, to share the insights and lessons I learned along the way so that more employees can be inspired. I hope that with the insights they would gain, they could avoid the business booby traps that are killing the dreams of many aspiring entrepreneurs.

It is my dream that more employees will take a leap of faith and become a certified *"Leapreneur."* You have the resources, the experience, and the passion to make it. All you need is inspiration and guidance, and I hope that this book will give you that. This is why I wrote this book for you.

What is Leapreneur

I've already mentioned "Leapreneur" in the previous page but we haven't actually defined it yet. Afterall, it's the title of this book so it might be good to know what it actually means.

Leapreneur is the word I personally coined from *"Leap of Faith"* and *"Entrepreneur."* You won't see it in the dictionary yet because I just invented it. However, I do hope that someday, more people will use it and it will be included in the Wikipedia, as a word that originates from the Philippines. ☺

The way I define Leapreneur is *"an employee who took the leap of faith to become a full-time entrepreneur."* So if you have a part-time business and still working as an employee, you are not a Leapreneur yet. You will only become a certified Leapreneur once you have taken the leap already by resigning from your job to become a full-time entrepreneur.

Most of the entrepreneurs I know are Leapreneurs. They started as employees first where they gained experience, then after few years, they started a part-time business before finally taking the leap as full-time entrepreneur.

This is the path that I recommend because it's safer, especially if you have no background in business yet. Here are some of the key benefits of becoming an employee first, before starting a business:

1.) You learn important skills and discipline that will be very helpful when you start your own business.

2.) You can use your savings from your salary as capital for your business.

3.) You build a network while working for a company that will be a huge advantage later on.

Unfortunately, despite being the preferred way of starting a business, there is no specific guide for employees on how to really start a business. Most books, trainings or seminars that are currently available are too generic that don't really address the unique situation and needs of employees who want to be entrepreneurs.

So this book is my own humble contribution in inspiring more employees to become *Leapreneurs*.

Your Key Takeaways

Write your key takeaways or learnings from the introduction.

Chapter 1: Building Your Entrepreneurial Mindset

Why I Left my 6-figure Salary to Start a Business

As I've shared with you in my story, I was really lucky to have worked for my first company. I was earning a 6-figure salary back then and travelling the world on paid business trips. I stayed in 5-star hotels and ate sumptuous food. I was working with the best people who always encouraged me to step up my game.

You can just imagine how difficult it was for some people to understand why I wanted to leave the corporate world. From the outside, it was a perfect career for me, and it's true. But inside, I longed for something different. Here are the reasons why:

1. Freedom

"I felt that even though I was earning that much, I was a slave to my work."

Every job has its light days and its stressful days. However, I vividly remember my breaking point. It was *Holy Thursday* (a holiday here in the Philippines) and my parents travelled for 10 hours from Bicol just to attend our much-awaited family vacation. We were supposed to travel to Batangas (a place with beautiful beaches, about 2 hours drive from Manila) by 9am that day to relax and bond as a family.

At 8am, I logged on to my computer and checked my email. When I was about to log out, my boss in Latin America messaged me and asked me to submit a report by 1pm that same day. Being the obedient employee that I am, I obliged because I knew how badly she needed the report.

My parents, brother, and sister were all ready to leave, except for me. They did not say anything but I felt their patience thinning after every hour that passed. Every minute that I spent doing that report meant fewer minutes to spend with my parents, who rarely came to Manila.

I submitted the report by 1pm and hurriedly ate lunch so we could go to Batangas already. On our way there, I felt so guilty and I said to myself that I didn't want to be a slave to my work anymore! I wanted more freedom!

This is our family picture in Batangas that day, April 13, 2006.

So beginning that day, I devoted more effort to Ink All-You-Can so that I could accelerate its success and be able to quit my corporate job faster.

2. Flexibility

"I wanted to bring my kids to school and go on family vacations whenever I wanted to."

That time, I wasn't married yet, though I did have officemates who had kids already. One of the common topics that we had during our lunch is the fact that they had trouble managing their time between work and family.

They wanted to bring their kids to school and attend important school events, but they couldn't because of work. One officemate recounted that the schedule of his 5-year old child is 12:00nn – 3:00pm. How could he possibly bring his kid to school with his fixed work schedule? In addition, his little boy was also playing basketball at 4 – 6pm. His kid had been begging him to watch his game but how could he? He said that he often struggled to explain to his kid why he missed those events, because when he says it's because of work, his kid will say, *"Na naman?! (Again?!)"*

I knew deep inside me that in a few years time, I will run into the same situation as theirs. So I said to myself, I need to do something about it now, before it's too late.

3. Financial Rewards
"I wanted to retire by age 45 without worrying about where to get our food and my kids' tuition fees."

I read this article about the *irony of time, energy and money.* It basically says that when we were kids, we had all the time and energy in the world but we didn't have money. When we grow up, we work very hard to earn money. It is during this phase of our lives that we focus too much on our work and tend to lose time for ourselves and for our family.

And then when the time comes for us to retire, we now have the *money* and we have the time to enjoy the fruits of our labor. Unfortunately, we don't have the energy anymore to enjoy it. *Low bat na, may arthritis, may high blood pa, at kung anu-ano pang limitations (Low battery already, with arthritis, with high blood pressure, plus a lot more limitations).* It struck me!

When can we then have the **time, energy, and money** to enjoy life?! I realized that if I don't make that conscious effort, I'll fall into that same trap. So I said to myself that I want to retire at 45 years old and I know that's just not possible if I continue as an employee.

4. Passion

"I want to explore, learn new things, and follow my passion."

While I was working for my first company, I had the privilege of being the first and only employee to be assigned to one of our company's distributors for nine (9) whole months. It was part of a sabbatical program initiated by our Finance Director in Asia. The distributor that I was assigned to had been incurring losses for several years already, and my objective was to make them profitable before the project ends.

To understand how to fix the huge problem of that distributor, I immersed myself in its operations. I got involved not just in accounting but also in sales, warehouse, logistics, etc. I rode the truck, joined the salesman to visit public markets, and met different sari-sari store owners. I learned how to sell products and run promotions for the stores.

Soon, I was able to implement the necessary changes that made that distributor not just profitable, *but one of the most profitable distributors* when my sabbatical finished. It was a great feeling of fulfillment that I couldn't forget.

That experience opened my eyes and made me realize that there is really more to me than just computing numbers and financial analysis. I got interested in learning new things and understanding how sales, marketing, warehouse, delivery, HR, etc. really work together to help a company move forward. I realized that I am bigger than my current work and I didn't want to be stuck there forever.

5. People

"I believe that I have the power to help at least 1 person eat 3 times a day."

Though I was earning much during that time, I also felt a responsibility to help other people. I had relatives who didn't have work. In the news, I saw people lining up every day under the heat of the sun trying to apply for a job. Every year, schools produced graduates who didn't know where to go.

Deep inside me, I believe that we have the power to help at least 1 person in our own little way. Not by giving them donations, but by giving them something more sustainable, like work. And if I can help just 1 person, it will make a huge impact in our country.

When I started, being an entrepreneur was *not as easy and as popular* as it is today. It was a time when once you started a business, people thought that you had been fired from your job or couldn't get any job at all. But no matter how intimidating starting a business was for me, I had to start doing it and learn as I went along!

I'm sure you've heard some or all of the reasons I've given. *But what about you? Why are you holding this book?* You might have similar or different reasons for wanting to become an entrepreneur.

No matter what your reasons are, one thing is for sure. If you don't take action, nothing will happen. Don't be like the other *wannapreneurs* out there who just dream and never have the guts to start the journey. Begin yours with reading this book and implementing what you will learn here...

What are the Differences between Employees and Entrepreneurs

Employees who go into business are often shocked by the world of entrepreneurship. They have difficulty transitioning because of certain mindsets they have as an employee.

So I looked at how I thought when I was still an employee and how I think now that I'm an entrepreneur. To be clear, the things that I will discuss here are my own reflections about me and some general observations. They may not be exactly true for you as an employee or an entrepreneur.

In this section, I'd like to share with you the observations I made through the years on how I think and act, when I was still an employee and now that I'm an entrepreneur.

1. Execution

While I was still working, I was typically obsessed with *"intellectualization"* and complicated data analysis. Before I submitted a project proposal, I had to do detailed financial analysis and it had to go through a series of reviews and approvals.

As an entrepreneur, on the other hand, I realized that market opportunities don't wait — by the time you've gotten all the information you need, the opportunity has passed already or somebody has taken over the market. Successful entrepreneurs decide and execute as soon as they realize there's a good chance of success. They don't wait for the product to be perfect because there's always a version 2.0.

2. Financial Resources

As an employee, I was generally blessed with generous budgets for assets, marketing, travel and accommodation, training, and even team-building. We had the best laptops, generous mobile phone plans, and stayed in carpeted offices and beautiful cubicles.

As an entrepreneur, on the other hand, I had to start with *zero budget*. If I can use my own printer to print my marketing materials, so be it. If I can find second-hand tables and chairs or get free online training, which is most welcome. Initially, I had to forego renting an office and just work at home or in the nearest coffee shop just to save on expenses. Every peso counts when you are an entrepreneur, because that peso is yours.

3. Risk Appetite

As an employee, I preferred proven and tested methodologies and processes. I was told *"Don't fix what ain't broken"* and to be comfortable with the current processes.

As an entrepreneur, I like to challenge the status quo and take risks. I always ask myself if there are better ways of doing things. Any savings or efficiencies will have direct impact on my bank balance. When I started my business, there were no set processes or methodologies yet so as an entrepreneur, I was encouraged to experiment.

4. Flexibility

While I was an employee, I preferred fixed and regular activities. I knew my exact routine every day and what to expect next month or next year.

Everything was planned ahead every year and changes were rarely made to those plans.

As an entrepreneur, I am constantly testing the plans every single day. I might have a P100 coupon this week but if it doesn't attract enough customers, I might increase it to P200 the following week. On the third week, the project might be totally scrapped. Things happen very fast in business and entrepreneurs thrive with these changes.

5. Knowledge & Experience

As an employee, I was often limited by my current skills. If I don't have experience with something, then I was afraid to do it. My knowledge then was also limited to the role I handled in the company, e.g. Audit, cost accounting, etc.

On the other hand, as an entrepreneur, I do not let a lack of knowledge, experience or talent get in the way of my success. When a good opportunity strikes, I say yes, learn on the job and grab the business before somebody takes it. Entrepreneurs, like me, are knowledgeable in the whole company operations and espouse continuous learning.

6. Source of Fulfillment

As an employee, I was motivated by job titles, praises from boss & salary increases. When I did a great job, I longed for praise from their boss.

I noticed that I'm more internally motivated as entrepreneur. When I do a great job, nobody praises me anymore but it's perfectly fine. Now, I get my satisfaction when people are happy using my products or services or when I reach my business goals. Though profit is a key factor for most entrepreneurs, some are just happy to earn a living as long as they are helping more people.

7. Diplomacy

As an employee, I worried too much about what people think so I tried to be diplomatic all the time. It's very rare in the corporate setting where you will see a manager scolding his subordinates.

As an entrepreneur, on the other hand, I am under incredible pressure to get results and save the business, so I take actions that are direct, in-your-face and (sometimes) unpleasant to the people around me. Even without any experience in Human Resource, I have to deal with reprimanding and firing people when necessary, just to save the business.

8. 15-30 and December 15

On a lighter note, as an employee, I always looked forward to important days like 15th / 30th of the month and most especially December 15th. However, as an entrepreneur, I dreaded the 15-30 and December 15 during my first few years because I didn't know where to get the cash to pay for the salaries and bonuses. There were cases where I had huge receivables from clients but on those important days, I needed cash.

What are the Characteristics of Successful Entrepreneurs

There are many characteristics of successful entrepreneurs. If we discuss them here, it could easily double the number of pages of this book. Thus, to make it simple, I'd like to highlight the four most important ones – *the mind, the eyes, the heart, and the hands.*

1. The Mind
"Unwavering Optimism and Perseverance"

Optimism and perseverance often make the difference between a successful entrepreneur and a failed one. In business, it doesn't matter how many times you fail, because you only need to be right once.

So you need to push through despite all the obstacles that are blocking your way. Most of the time, these hindrances are just tests of how badly you really want something. Most successful entrepreneurs didn't just triumph after one try. They experienced a series of failures but they never gave up. They see failure as a component of success and an opportunity to start all over again. They believe that if there is a will, there's a way.

In an article published in the *Harvard Business Review*, researchers from Lund University in Sweden, found that *"In simple terms, our results suggest that entrepreneurs view the future as bright—but they are actually right. Our evidence thereby challenges the prevailing argument that entrepreneurs are irrational in how they form their beliefs about the future. Rather, it is non-entrepreneurs who are more irrational, because their beliefs are overly pessimistic."*

2. The Eyes
"Clear Vision"

Entrepreneurs are very clear on what they want to get accomplished long-term. It may seem like they are doing things at random, but they are not. They know exactly how it will fit together in the end.

Once they set their eyes on the goal, it's very hard to distract them from achieving it. They become focused and single-minded on what they want. They captivate the imagination of everyone when they share this vision. As a result, they are able to get the commitment and support of employees and business partners because of this clear vision of the future.

3. The Heart
"Contagious Passion"

Successful entrepreneurs have contagious passion about what they are doing. In fact, they can talk for hours non-stop about their business and their energy level will never wane. It is through this passion that the entrepreneur gets all his energy and determination to succeed.

To get this passion, entrepreneurs don't just choose random business ideas to pursue. They pursue businesses that they have a lot of interest in, something that they love and want to share with other people. Their passion overflows and becomes contagious.

4. The Hands
"Action Oriented"

Entrepreneurs are masters of execution. They execute and deliver fast, and avoid falling into the trap of over-analyzing things. In fact, they think that everything is an experiment so they test their assumptions and revise their plans accordingly.

Most entrepreneurs take calculated risks, not blind risks. Entrepreneurs understand that nothing great will happen if you don't take risks and take action. Entrepreneurs believe that there is always uncertainty and a possibility of failure in any situation so this never fazes them to take action.

Recent developments in the Lean Start-up Strategy underscores the importance of releasing *"just good enough product"* and not wait for it to be perfect because there's always a version 2.0. This way, entrepreneurs can test the business already without spending too much time and money.

Top 10 Common Misconceptions About Entrepreneurship

Aspiring entrepreneurs have a lot of misconceptions about business and entrepreneurship. Before I go any further, let me discuss them briefly. I'll not go into details yet because I will cover them anyway throughout the book.

1. "I am too young or too old to be an entrepreneur."

There is no one too young or too old for business, especially in this modern world. Anyone can be a successful entrepreneur anytime. It is even possible to become billionaires at the age of 27. Take it from the founders of Facebook, Mark Zuckerberg ($17.5 billion) and Dustin Moskovitz ($3.5 billion).

There are even retirees who successfully became entrepreneurs. In business, age doesn't matter. It's the attitude, willingness to learn, and bias for action that makes the difference. Of course, the sooner you get started, the better your chances are based on the 10,000-Hour-Rule.

2. Most entrepreneurs are overnight successes.

Sometimes, we get too overwhelmed or excited to earn that we forget nothing happens overnight. Most successful entrepreneurs have their own share of hardships and trials. It takes a lot of hard work and determination to become successful in business.

For example, convincing customers to buy your product vs. a competitor is hard. Getting employees who *"really care"* about your company is also hard. So you have to work through those stumbling blocks, if you want to become successful.

3. All you need is a great idea to succeed.

To reiterate, success as an entrepreneur takes 90 percent perspiration and 10 percent inspiration (your business idea). No matter how great your product or service is, it will not penetrate your chosen market without real hard work.

4. It's better to start a new or innovative product that no one is selling yet.

As I will discuss in the succeeding chapters, introducing a new product and creating an industry around it is *not for first-time entrepreneurs*. Those products typically require a lot of time and money to educate the customers, so beware.

When you find a great idea and no one else is doing it anywhere in the world, that's a red flag. We can't possibly be too brilliant that we were the first one to think about it, especially if we don't have any business experience yet. This means either the market is not big enough or it's too expensive to reach the target customers.

5. Entrepreneurs are born, not made.

Wake up! No one is born an entrepreneur. The knowledge and skills about running a business are learned. It's definitely an advantage if you are exposed to the business environment early on in your life but if not, you can still learn how to do it.

6. I must be good in sales and marketing to be an entrepreneur.

I must admit, being good in sales and marketing is a big advantage when you start your own business. This is because that task of getting the first few customers generally falls into your hands. You have to be able to sell your products and your company well, not just to your customers, but also to your prospective employees. Being able to articulate your vision will inspire your employees.

On the other hand, anything can be learned as long as you are willing to do it.

7. Entrepreneurs have more time for their selves and their family.

Didn't I just say that it's one of the reasons why I started my own business – to have the freedom and flexibility that I want? Well, this one should be qualified. During the first few years of your business, it's less likely that you will have more time for yourself and family. Most probably, you will work harder than ever before, doing business-related tasks at night and during weekends.

However, I look at it as an investment. When you've built the business and made it sustainable, that's when you can enjoy the fruits of your labor and have more time for your family.

8. Entrepreneurs are geniuses.

I wish I could be called a genius along with other entrepreneurs. But we are not. We are just ordinary people who are passionate about our products and services.

In fact, when you look at your batch mates, you might observe that the entrepreneurs in your batch are not necessarily the smartest people in your class. They just have average intelligence but are really *"street-smart" or "madiskarte (resourceful)"* and *"malakas ang loob (courageous)."* The good news is that these things can be learned through practice. ☺

9. You always have to offer the lowest price to win.

Most first-time entrepreneurs have the wrong notion that they need to offer the lowest price to win. I'm not a believer of that. Low prices are only for big companies like Walmart and other retailers who have deep pockets to sustain their business. Unfortunately, we don't have that many resources to begin with.

For me, customers don't necessarily look for the cheapest price, especially for niche products and services. They look for "value for money." That means product quality and excellent service come into play.

When you offer the lowest price, you undermine your quality and service. This is the reason why the prices of our ink refills are 2x the prices of our competitors. We stand for quality and service, not price.

10. To be an entrepreneur, you have to risk it all.

Yes, taking risks is important if you want to be an entrepreneur. You can't possibly start a business without risking anything, even your time at the very least.

However, you don't have to risk it all. That's what this book is all about. I'm going to teach you how to be mitigate the risks and learn from my mistakes so you minimize your losses. Starting a business should be done cautiously, not arrogantly.

What's Holding Back Employees from Becoming Entrepreneurs

A lot of employees want to go into business but they worry so much about too many things. Worrying too much freezes them and they get stuck where they are. After years and years, nothing has happened.

In this section, I'd like to share my thoughts on the common things that hold employees back from becoming entrepreneurs. I hope that I will be able to provide some clarity and advice in case you are in this situation.

1. Lack of Funds or Initial Capital

Employees often complain that they do not have enough savings to start a business. Their salary apparently is just enough to support all their basic needs. So if they will start a business, they need to borrow money or sell their property.

Most of the time, we just need to be creative and smart with how we start a business. I was inspired recently by the show of *Carl Balita, Radyo Negosyo in DZMM.* They have a contest where Carl challenges the listeners to start their own business with just P500.

Amazingly, I've heard many success stories where a business idea bloomed with just P500 initial capital. This goes to show that you don't have to invest huge amounts of money to get started in business. As I always say, *"Dream big, but spend small."*

In *Chapter 2 – Getting Ideas for your Business*, we will discuss the types of businesses that you can start with minimal capital to get the ball rolling. We will also discuss in *Chapter 3 – Testing your Business Idea* how you can evaluate your ideas properly to minimize your capital exposure.

2. Lack of Time

One of the most common barriers for employees who want to start their business is a lack of time. It's a given that we already work at least 40 hours each week for our full-time jobs plus an additional 10 hours for travel time.

However, I believe that if you really want to engage into business, you'll find time for it just like how you find time for your family and friends. No matter how demanding your work and family are, you can always squeeze a little time here and there to make way for your goal. I have done it, and so have other entrepreneurs.

To help you out, turn to *Chapter 4 – Managing Your Business Part-time and for the First Time* where I will share my schedule when I was starting my business to give you an idea as to how I did it. I will also share my tips and tricks on how to manage your business and work at the same time.

3. Lack of Experience or Training

It's true that employees often lack the experience and training when it comes to running a business. They are clueless at knowing where to start. This is because unlike most Chinese businessmen who expose their children to their business, most employees come from the *"working class"* and have parents who are not entrepreneurs. Thus, they did not grow up in a business-oriented environment.

The way I look at it is like wanting to drive a car but not knowing how to drive. So what do you do? Do you just give up? No! You learn how to drive, as simple as that. Starting a business is the same thing. We can learn how to do it if we really want to.

The good news is that the Entrepreneur Community is now solid and supportive, unlike 15 years ago when I was just starting out. There are many seminars and meet-ups where you can meet fellow entrepreneurs.

Let's not forget, grabbing a copy of this book is the first step. I want to *congratulate* you for investing in this book. This is packed with tips and insights that I learned during my 15 years of being an entrepreneur. Keep it up and continue reading because there's still a lot more to learn!

4. Fear to Change the Status Quo

Corporate employees have a steady flow of income every month. They are comfortable with their job, their officemates, their boss, and their company. Their schedule is predictable, as well as the issues they encounter. In short, they are living in their comfort zone.

But what will happen if you start a business? It's something unknown that makes you panic. That's why I wrote a book about my journey from employee to entrepreneur--to shed more light on what really happens when you take the leap. Hopefully, by reading this book, you'll be inspired to take action.

For me, we owe it to ourselves and our family to change for the better, especially if we can do it! For example, if we can afford to send our kids to a better school, then why not do it? If we can move to a bigger house, why not? So if starting a business means we can live a better life, why not?!

5. Fear of Failure

Who wants to fail? Nobody. It's a shame if you quit your job, start a business, and then fail miserably. Afterwards, you swallow your pride and go knocking on your employer's door for a job, and your family members don't have anything to say but *"We told you so."*

That's why you have to lessen the risk of starting a business. I don't recommend that you quit your job tomorrow. In fact, I highly recommend that you start a part-time business first, as you learn how to do it. When your business can already support your financial needs, then that's the time that you can quit your job.

Just to be clear though, failure is a component of success, as I've shared with you in my business insights. Be prepared to fail. There is no shortcut there. But with the help of this book, I will teach you how to minimize your failures. It's okay to be afraid, but don't let it stop you from reaching your goal.

Why You Should Stop Making Excuses

In Malcolm Gladwell's Book *"Outliers,"* he studied the lives of extremely successful people to find out how they achieved success. He examined the causes of why the majority of Canadian ice hockey players are born in the first few months of the calendar year, how Microsoft co-founder *Bill Gates* achieved his extreme wealth, how *The Beatles* became one of the most successful musical acts in human history, and more.

He said that the *key to success in any field is to practice for roughly ten thousand hours*.   This is the *"10,000-Hour Rule."*

If you will spend 20–30 hours per week on your part-time business, how long will it take you to achieve 10,000 hours? Let's do the math:

Total Time Needed:
$$= 10,000 \text{ Hrs} / 25 \text{ ave. hrs per week}$$
$$= 400 \text{ weeks} / 52 \text{ weeks per year}$$
$$= 7 \text{ years and 8 months}$$

This means in order to become good in business, it will take 7 years and 8 months, assuming you spend 25 hours per week as a part-time entrepreneur. Thus, if you are 25 right now, you'll be *32 years old* when you can call yourself an expert. If you are 30 years old now, you'll be 37 years old. If you are 40 years old now, you'll be 47 years old by the time you get good at the trade.

If you think about it, the children who were exposed to business early on began their training when they were still young. That's why when they graduated from college, they can immediately jump into entrepreneurship and become successful. They had more than 10,000 hours already.

But for ordinary people like us who were not born with a family business and don't have any business background, we are starting from scratch! So that means that the sooner you take action, the better. That is, unless you want to wait to be a senior citizen first before becoming good in business.

As soon as I began working for my first company, I also started setting-up my own business on the side. That was in the year 2000. I've already shared that I failed 3 times and I started Ink All-You-Can in 2005 as my 4th attempt in business. In 2007, I finally took the leap of faith and became a full-time *leapreneur*.

Wait a minute! If you think about it, it actually took me 5 years of practice to start a profitable business. In fact, it took me 7 years before I was able to finally quit my job. Was it the 10,000-Hour-Rule that Malcolm Gladwell was talking about? I don't know, maybe it was just a coincidence.

I shared this insight to my friends who also started their own businesses from scratch (meaning without prior knowledge on running a business). The funny thing was they told me that it also took them between 5 – 7 years of practice before they finally made it big as entrepreneurs. Maybe there's really some truth about Gladwell's theory after all. But nevertheless, I urge you to start now!

Why I persisted after Failing 3 Times

I had 3 painful experiences with business failures. I experienced the excitement of conceptualizing a new business idea to the point that I can't stop thinking about it and would lose sleep over it. After I executed it and I failed, the combined feeling of loss, worry, and determination was something that I couldn't describe.

Many people asked me where I got the courage to continue my dream even after failing 3 times and losing more than P1M. They said that if they lost P50,000, it would be very hard for them to recover and they might give up already.

Looking back, it was really a very bold move for me to push through despite everything that happened. I tried to recall what I was thinking during that time. I asked myself, *"Why was I so focused on my goal that I persisted even after failing 3 times?"* Here are the answers that came up:

1) I believed that this is part of my "tuition fee" in learning the business.

Since I didn't have any formal education or mentors on how to start a business, I was doing it the best way I knew how. Due to my inexperience, I made mistakes along the way but I also picked up valuable lessons that made me become a better entrepreneur.

I considered the losses as my tuition fees in learning how to run a business. I said to myself that if I wanted to learn, I had to make sacrifices that may include paying for mistakes in order to get valuable lessons in return.

2) I felt that there is NO WAY I will fail forever, so I just have to keep trying.

Though I was bruised and down, I did not give up. It felt like the saying *"habang nasusugatan, lalong tumatapang (as you get wounded, you become braver)."* I truly believed that there is no way I will fail forever. It's just a matter of time and I will eventually become successful.

So whenever I was hurt, I just said to myself *"Pasasaan ba't tatamaan ko rin yan! (In time, I will hit it right!)"* And on the 4th try, I was right!

3) I believed that my dream is worth more than what I lost.

Every time I lost, my dream of being able to bring the kids to school, have freedom to do what I want, and retire early flashed in my mind. I want those dreams so badly and I was willing to pay more than P1M just to fulfill those dreams.

What about you? How much are you willing to pay to make your dreams come true? P10,000? P100,000? P1,000,000? Or whatever it takes?!

What's Next?

In the next chapter, *Getting Ideas for your Business*, we will discuss how you can get inspiration for your business ideas.

We will also discuss the difference between franchising and starting your own business concept, as well as my suggestion on which one is the safer route.

Lastly, we will go through the examples of businesses that are safer for first-time entrepreneurs like online business, skill-based businesses, hobbies, and many more.

Your Key Takeaways

Write your key takeaways or learnings from this chapter.

Chapter 2: Getting Ideas for Your Part-time Business

How to Get Inspiration for Your Business Ideas

Getting inspiration for your business ideas should be an easy process. After talking to a lot of employees who want to be entrepreneurs, I realized that most of them already had business ideas. In fact, some of them had multiple ideas that they were considering.

So, I think there is really no shortage of business ideas. What is lacking is probably the courage to **_start doing something_** about that idea. Unless you execute it, it will be useless, no matter how brilliant the idea is.

However, in case you still don't have that big idea in your head, don't worry. We will cover that in this section. Here are the quick tips on how to get inspiration for your business idea:

1. Analyze Your Professional Skills.
What are you good at? Are you good at public speaking, research, or graphic design? Can you use it to start your business? This is a very easy way to start a business.

As we will discuss later in the chapter, you can sell your services online in freelancing websites to get started. You can also offer consulting services to companies who might need your specific skills.

Case-In-Point

We have an employee who is good at making PowerPoint Presentations. What he did is offer his services to freelancing websites like www.freelancer.com and www.elance.com.

On a typical month, he earns around P8,000 on the side by simply making PowerPoint presentations. Not bad for a part-time business done on your spare time, right?

How about you? Do you have skills that you can also sell to other people?

Note that this is _not_ necessarily the business that you will grow old with. This can just be an _easy way to get started_ on your business without spending money. Best of all, the learning and insights that you will get here, like how to get clients and how to price your service, will be invaluable later on for your other business ideas.

2. Review Your Past Experiences.

We've all been customers of different products and services. Can you recall what irritated or frustrated you the most? Maybe you availed of a service and complained about something but the staff told you that's not how they do it there. Or perhaps you are looking for a special variation of a product that you spent hours going to a far and unfamiliar place just to get the product that you want.

If there are more people like you who want that product, a business idea just might be hiding there.

Can you do something about it and make it a business?

3. Check Your Hobbies

This is also one of the easiest ways to start a business. It normally doesn't need huge capital and you are already very familiar with the product or service already.

Are you good at baking? How about making jewelry or accessories? Do you love training dogs? Maybe you can offer them to your friends, and later on, to other people. You can also explore selling informative products like e-books where you share your recipe or secrets to those who want to be good at that skill like you.

I have a friend who is good at making different kinds of accessories. Recently, she discovered Villalobos Street in Quiapo, Manila. It's the place to go if you want to source materials like beads, Swarovski crystals, pearls, pendants, charms, etc. All the stores in that street sell those items so you really have a wide selection to choose from and a good bargaining power.

What she did was to offer her specially-designed bouquet to soon-to-be brides. As we all know, it's a lucrative niche that is growing every year. That market is hungry for new ideas to make their weddings even more special.

With a budget of less than P3,000 and a weekend to spare, my friend was able to start a simple business borne out of a hobby, earning her P5,000 – P10,000 per project.

4. Visit Tradeshows

Tradeshows and Business Expos are excellent venues for keeping yourself abreast with the latest trends and products in the market. You will normally see different businesses selling their new products during the tradeshow. It's also easy to spot which ones attract the most visitors.

This is also the perfect venue to talk to a business owner/entrepreneur, or at least to the head of marketing or operations. You can get a lot of inspiration and inside information simply by talking to them.

In the early 2000's, I made sure to attend all the business expos to get inspiration on what business I could start. One of the tradeshows that I regularly visited was the Annual Filipino Franchise Show organized by AFFI, an association of Filipino entrepreneurs. They have been organizing that show since 1997.

When Ink All-You-Can became successful, I immediately joined the AFFI and became an exhibitor in their trade show. It was like a dream come true because I can still vividly remember the time when I was just a visitor, looking for a business to start. Then, this 2015, I was elected as the President of AFFI where I had the privilege of recommending different programs to help aspiring entrepreneurs. From a visitor, to an exhibitor, then to the Presidency of AFFI, time really flies fast if you enjoy what you are doing.

5. Check out Alibaba.com

In case you are wondering what product to sell or where to source products from China, you can check out www.alibaba.com. I bet you can find all the items that you are looking for there, from electronics, equipment, toys, apparels, to supplies and more. It's the haven of different suppliers. They have recently become famous with their record-breaking initial public offering worth $25 billion in New York Stock Exchange last September 2014.

Just a word of caution though. There are scammers there, so be careful. I was once scammed by an agent there. After I paid, she said she already shipped the product and provided me with a tracking number. But when I received it, it was a cheap item that I did not order. After that, she suddenly disappeared. Take caution and go for reliable suppliers!

6. Visit Online forums and websites
There are a lot of online forums and websites that you can get ideas from. Just Google for business forums and start reading.

Most magazines also have an online presence where you can read helpful articles without spending anything.

Sites like www.entrepreneur.com.ph can give you a lot of business ideas. Recently, they've also boosted their efforts on promoting start-up business ideas like how to make custom-designed chocolates, how to make yema cake, how to make siomai, etc.

7. Monitor Press Releases and Ads
You can also monitor press releases and advertisements in newspapers, magazines, and websites to get business ideas. Typically, businesses release press statements and place ads when they introduce new products or offer new services.

Once you are interested in a certain industry, you can research the key players and read their website and press releases. You can gain a lot of insights simply by doing a few clicks here and there.

When you see new products or services ask yourself these questions:

   a) Why are they introducing this new product or service? Who is the intended market?
   b) What business insight can I get out of this?
   c) Are there other industries or target markets where I can apply this insight and create a business out of it?

The easiest way to assess if a product is making money or not is to monitor their ad spending. If you constantly see the same ad being run over and over again in newspapers and magazines, you can safely bet that it is working and the company is making money. Otherwise, they would not spend another Peso on those expensive ads if they were not working. Makes sense?

What ads have you observed lately that pops up over and over again? Is there a business idea there worth exploring?

8. Observe Successful Businesses

When I go to the malls or any commercial area, I don't just shop but I also observe other businesses. I want to know what the new shops are and which ones closed their stores. I also look at the new promotions or marketing campaigns of other stores, as well as check which ones are busy entertaining customers and which ones are dying to get one. Given a chance, I also talk to the sales staff to get more information, like the store's best sellers and who usually buys those products.

With this simple technique, I get a feel for what is happening with the market, not just for my industry, but also for other industries that I might learn from. You can also do this to get inspiration for your business.

Should you Buy a Franchise or Start on Your Own

Franchising is a growing industry, not just here in the Philippines, but globally as well. For entrepreneurs who have a proven business model, it is the fastest way to expand without needing huge capital and going through management headaches.

For franchisees, they get a chance to own a business with a proven business model and well-recognized brand. This minimizes trial and errors in business and that's why franchise businesses have a higher success rate than starting on your own.

When thinking about franchising or starting your own business, I'd like to summarize the key differences in simple terms so you can easily remember them. Below are the things you need to consider:

1. Risk

Getting a franchise is definitely less risky compared to starting on your own. This is because Franchisors already have proven business models that work and can be replicated in other locations. They also have established their brands and have marketing support that you can capitalize on to grow your business.

When you start on your own, you have to do all the work in developing a profitable business model that you can eventually expand later on. This is risky especially if you are a first-time entrepreneur.

2. Time to Set-up

When you get a typical franchise, you can generally start operating in about 2 - 3 months. After passing the franchisee screening process, the Franchisor can assist you with the site evaluation, conduct your training, set-up branch immersion, and prepare the inventory and supplies that you will need. Franchising is really a shortcut for those who want to start a business.

If you start on your own, it may take longer, especially if you are doing it part-time. You have to start from scratch: from researching the product or service, sourcing it out, testing the pricing, creating the brand, finding locations, to opening the store. Since you don't have the business experience and network yet, it could even take much longer.

3. Investment

The investment in a franchise is typically higher, compared to setting up your own business. However, if you don't know what you are doing, starting a business on your own may prove to be more expensive in the long run.

In terms of absolute amount though, you need at least P150,000 to get a reputable franchise. A franchise of established brands like Jollibee can even fetch up to P25M – P30M. Most people don't have that amount of money, so franchising may be a turn-off for them.

4. Operation & Logistics

The franchise package already includes *Standard Operating Procedures* (SOPs) with built-in controls. Some packages even include sales and inventory software, CCTV and timekeeping devices.

These tools help make the operation of the franchise very manageable.

You also don't have to worry about suppliers and deliveries because the franchisor takes care of them. In short, it's like a turn-key business that you can operate more easily compared to starting on your own.

5. Flexibility & Control

In terms of flexibility and control with the business, you don't have much choice but to follow the standards of the Franchisor. If you are a franchisee of Jollibee, for example, you can't just change the taste of spaghetti or add *"lugaw (porridge)"* to your menu. You can't even run promotions on your own, unless you get clearance from your Franchisor.

On the other hand, you can tweak whatever you want in your own business. If you don't want the logo anymore, you can change or refresh it anytime. Do you want to extend the warranty to get more sales? Just go ahead. The only downside of flexibility though is that you might be changing the wrong things or even making things worse, so just be careful.

6. Profit

The good thing about a franchise is that you are buying a proven business model. There is a higher chance that you will earn, though there is no guarantee. However, the profit is usually capped or limited. It can give you predictable profit but it cannot make you really rich, unless you get more franchises.

If you own the business and hit the jackpot, you can franchise it to other entrepreneurs and expand to 100 branches or more. Franchising will multiply your profits and you are only capped by your own imagination and perseverance.

To summarize our discussion above, there are big advantages to getting a franchise compared to starting on your own, especially for first-time entrepreneurs. You can refer to the matrix below for easy reference:

Area	Franchising	On Your Own
Time to Set-up	Short	Long
Investment	High	Low
Risk	Low	High
Operations & Logistics	Easy	Hard
Flexibility & Control	Less	More
Profits	Limited	Unlimited

My Recommendations

So what do I recommend, after seeing both worlds (starting on my own business and failing three (3) times and now I'm a franchisor)? Here is my two cents worth of advice for first-time entrepreneurs or those employees who want to go into business:

If you have limited amount of capital, say P100,000 or less:

   a) **Start with a Service Business First** - If you have limited amount of capital, I suggest that you start with a service business first. If you are good in marketing, accounting, web design, writing, etc., offer your services to other companies as a freelancer.

This way, you don't have to worry about inventory, rent, payroll, etc. that often kills first-time entrepreneurs. All you have to worry is to promote your services online or through your network, and slowly grow from there.

Please refer to the next section *"Safer Businesses for First-time Entrepreneurs"* for more examples of the types of businesses that you can easily start.

b) ***Save Your Earnings from the Business*** – Whatever you earn from this business, do not touch it. Do not buy new phones or gadgets! Save it in a separate bank account so you won't be tempted to spend it.

You can only use the money to reinvest in the business by promoting it to get more clients. Otherwise, save it so you can use it later on as capital for your new business.

c) ***Grow Your Service Business or Move on to the Second Business*** – Promote your business and grow it as much as you can handle. Do not start a business until you fully maximized your income from this business.

There might come a time that you need to hire an employee to help you with the business. Don't rush it. It will just come naturally.

d) ***Move on to the Second Business*** – Once you have fully maximized the first business and you have saved enough capital, you may start a second business. This can be a franchise or your own product.

<u>If you have enough capital, like more than P100,000 – P1,000,000 to invest in a business:</u>

a) ***Get a Franchise First*** - If you have the money to spare, get a franchise first. It will teach you a lot of things about running a business.

   However, make sure that you specifically discuss with the franchisor if they already have success stories of franchisees who are managing the business part-time. Ask them for names and make sure that you talk to those franchisees so you get an idea if the franchise business can really be managed part-time.

b) ***Study How the Business Operates*** – Skills like pricing, sales and marketing will be very helpful when you start your own business. Make sure that you also build your relationship with your Franchisor and fellow franchisees.

c) ***Start Looking for Another Business*** – After operating the franchise for 1 – 2 years, you may start looking for a new business that you can start on your own. Don't start too early because you will get distracted and your franchise business will suffer.

d) ***Build your Own Business*** – While still operating the franchise, build your own business. Ask advice from your franchisor and other franchisees how to do it. They will most likely be open to helping you out since you have the relationship and it's not competing with their business anyway.

e) ***Be A Franchisor*** - Once you have at least 5 successful branches, start thinking of franchising on your own to expand your business. Just make sure that you have a solid foundation and business model already to avoid any backlash. A lot of companies fail because they expand too fast.

A Word about Franchise Scams

Before we proceed, I'd like to advise you to beware of scams that offer *"too-good-to-be-true"* franchises. Check the background of the owner and the company first, talk to their franchisees, and assess the feasibility of their offer and business model. Don't be too excited to give a down payment without exercising due diligence.

I've heard so many stories of people who invested their hard-earned money only to be defrauded by dishonest companies. In fact, the *Department of Trade and Industry* (DTI) has issued a ruling that companies who franchise their business must be a member of a franchise organization, like AFFI and PFA, to protect the public interest. To learn more about franchising, you can visit www.affi.com.ph

What are the Safer Businesses for First-time Entrepreneurs

For first-time entrepreneurs, here are some examples of the types of businesses that you can start on a part-time basis:

Online Businesses

On-line businesses are perhaps one of the easiest and cheapest businesses that you can start on the side. Selling and marketing can be done online, while delivery of the product or service can be offline.

Here are some examples of on-line businesses:

1. Sell Products Online

You can sell niche products online that are not readily available in malls. Just imagine, while other retailers are limited by their branches or physical locations, you can practically sell across the Philippines, and even in other countries. Here are some quick tips in finding the right product to sell on-line.

a) Focus on a niche product that is not readily available in malls and supermarkets. A delicacy or hand-made products are good examples of this.
b) Make sure that it is small and light enough to be packed and shipped across the country. Stay away from products that are fragile or require special handling like chemicals or inks.
c) Make sure there is consistent demand for the product throughout the year, unless you really just want to do it for a few months. Thus, avoid seasonal products like Christmas décor or

Halloween costumes because you might end up with unsold inventory after the season.

d) Avoid those products that require after-sales support because it will be hard to cater to them especially when they are located in another city.

e) Make sure you can sell it with enough margin, e.g. at least 2x-4x the cost of the product.

2. E-books and Webinars

Did you know that Amazon declared that in 2012, the sales of e-books sold surpassed the sales of physical books? Back in 2008, the sales of e-books in the US alone is worth $500M. But in 2014, that amount reached to $5.6B or more than 10x in the last 6 years.

You can also get a tiny slice of this market by creating informative products. The good thing about this business is that your e-cash register will continue to ring, even when you are at work or on vacation.

Tim Ferris, author of the best-selling book *"The 4-hour Work Week"*, has written a very good article about how to write e-books entitled "How to (Really) Make $1,000,000 Selling E-Books." It has real-world case studies so make sure you check it out in this link. I also encourage you to subscribe to his blog to get more insights and inspiration.

3. Blogging

If you are a writer, you can create your own blog to start getting online traction. Setting up a blog is easy. However, getting visitors is the harder part.

Here is a nice guide on how to start your own blog in case you are interested. Take note however, that you will need at least 1 – 3 years before you can earn decent income from blogging. So it takes a lot of discipline, perseverance, and hardwork. If you are not a natural writer, I won't recommend this route.

4. Virtual Assistant

As a virtual assistant, you can do data encoding and data entry, online research, transcription, etc. It's enticing business because you have a flexible schedule, you can work in comfortable clothes, and best of all, you don't have to bear the burden of horrific traffic every day.

According to Elance-oDesk, the largest company for online freelance services in the world, their Philippine operations alone generate more than US$200 million (PHP9 billion) in income annually, while globally, revenues reach over $900 million. That's a big industry to be in.

You can also check out www.upwork.com and www.freelancer.com to get started.

Franchise Businesses

We had a detailed discussion about franchising in the previous section. One of its biggest advantages is that it has proven business model and the standards and systems are already in place. Thus, managing a franchise business becomes much easier such that you can do it part-time.

For a list of franchise businesses that you can consider, you can go to www.entrepreneur.com.ph and www.affi.com.ph.

Skill-based Businesses

Most of us have developed certain skills because of our education and training. These skills can be used as a starting point when we want to build our own business.

Here are some examples of skill-based businesses:

1. Training and Consulting

Training and consulting is one of the lucrative businesses that you can start using the professional skills that you developed over time. The reason for this is that you can price it according to whatever you want, as long as you justify it well.

For example, you can do sales training for P3,000 or you can charge hundreds of millions of pesos for a training session. It really depends on how good you are and how you sell yourself. This is the reason why some motivational speakers can _charge one hundred thousand per hour_.

Some other training or consulting ideas include:
a) Excel Training
b) Digital Marketing Training/Consulting
c) HR and Organization Development Training/Consulting
d) English Tutoring for Speakers of Other Languages
e) Tutoring for elementary and high school students

2. Accounting, Tax, and Bookkeeping

You can offer accounting or bookkeeping services to companies or entrepreneurs. Most entrepreneurs are too busy running their business so they need help in managing the financials.

I met an accountant (not a CPA), who offered his services to entrepreneurs for P3,000–P5,000 every month. His services only covered the filing of Value-Added Tax Returns, Withholding Tax Returns, and Pag-ibig and Social Security System (SSS) every month, even though they can be filed online.

From the entrepreneur's point of view, it's the comfort that you are doing it right and that you can get advice from an experienced accountant that makes the services worth it.

---

3. Graphics Design and Desktop Publishing

If you are good at graphic design, you can offer your services in the freelancing websites that I mentioned earlier. Additionally, you can also join www.99designs.com to bid for design projects like logos, brochures, websites, and even mobile app designs.

4. Writing

Writing is one of the most sought-after skills in online freelancing. In order to get higher rankings in search engines, companies need to produce high-quality content for their blogs and websites. They need to engage their customers by sharing helpful tips and inspiring stories. That's why more and more companies need extra help in developing content.

I, for one, need eligible writers to develop articles and helpful tips for our different websites. If you are good at writing, I need your services.

5. Event Planning and Hosting

For those good at project management or hosting events, you may have a business idea waiting to be tapped. You can organize weddings, birthday parties, and even small corporate events like product launches and anniversary events.

You can offer your services to your friends first and then get referrals from your satisfied clients. I have a friend who hosts weddings and she is paid P10,000 for a few hours work. Best of all, most weddings are done on weekends so it doesn't affect her full-time work!

6. Software Programming

Given the rise of mobile phones, app development has become in-demand in recent years. Moreover, when you develop an app, you can easily charge hundreds of thousands because not so many developers know how to do it yet. Companies are willing to pay a hefty amount so they can reach their mobile customers.

So if you have this skill, work on it further and earn from it while it's still hot!

Hobbies

Hobbies are also a good source of business ideas that you can start with limited capital. Some examples are:

1. Baking Cakes and Pastries

You can bake cakes, cupcakes, brownies, and other pastries. These are especially popular during events like birthdays, anniversaries, and Christmas.

Nowadays, cake pops are becoming very popular in parties because it's easy to eat and distribute. A cake pop is a form of cake styled as a lollipop. It was first popularized by a blogger, www.bakerella.com.

We have done it with our kids and they absolutely love it. In fact, we are planning to serve it during the birthday party of our son. We tried looking for suppliers and we found someone offering it on www.olx.ph for P35.00 per piece. Based on our computation when we made the cake pops ourselves, it roughly costs P5.00 per piece only. That means P30.00 profit for a very simple business that is advertised for free.

---

2. Diet-based Meals

These are becoming popular lately. With the growing problem of high cholesterol, artery blockages, and other dreadful health problems, the demand for healthy meals is on the rise.

If you like cooking and you're a fan of certain diet programs, you can definitely make a business out of it. You can promote your product online and in food bazaars to help get the word out.

There are online sites now in the Philippines that specializes in delivering different meals to customers, like the No-carb Diet, South Beach Diet, Paleo Diet, etc. When you check out their sites, their prices start from P3,000 to P7,000 per week.

You can check out www.thesexychef.ph and www.paleomanila.com to see how it works.

Can you localize the service and make a twist on their business model?

---

3. Custom Jewellery and Accessories Making

Finally, your high grade in art class will come in handy. You can make custom jewellery and other accessories and sell it to your friends or online.

I have friends who are making money selling custom jewellery and accessories on her Facebook page and Instagram account. You can visit Villalobos Street in Quiapo to source materials.

4. Photography or Videography

You can offer your services to restaurants, small businesses and brands that are into franchising. Most of these companies need high quality product shots and a nice company video for their website and other marketing collaterals. It makes their marketing message more compelling.

Don't go to saturated markets like weddings and birthday parties. Instead, look for a niche that you can dominate. By the way, you can also try selling your shots on stock photo websites like www.shutterstock.com and www.istockphotos.com and earn a commission for every downloaded file.

Other Part-time Businesses

The following are some more examples of businesses that you can start while you are working:

1. T-Shirt, Mug, Invitation and other Printing Services

People just can't get enough of t-shirts and mugs and that's why this remains an attractive business, even though it peaked a few years ago here in the Philippines. It's relatively inexpensive to start a small-scale operation using just a printer, heat-transfer paper and a heat press.

2. Soap, Scented Candles, and Perfume-Making

Whether it's a relaxing bubble bath, a soothing foot scrub, or the calming smell of scented oil, many women long for a spa experience right in their home. So if you share this same passion, consider starting a business creating soaps, perfumes, lotions and other spa products that you can sell to your friends, officemates and relatives.

There are hundreds of free and helpful tutorials online showing you how to start your business with P3,000 or less.

3. Direct Selling

When I was still studying in college, one of my friends was selling Avon products to our classmates. She earned good commission from doing it part-time. Avon is said to be the number 1 direct-selling company in the Philippines. Other examples of direct-selling companies include Boardwalk, Mary Kay, Natasha, and Amway.

One good thing about joining direct-selling companies is that you get excellent training on sales, marketing, and personality development. They invest in developing their agents/representatives because they make money through your efforts.

So even if you don't reach your financial goals with direct-selling, you will at least get real-world training that you can use for your own business.

4. Insurance

Insurance agents typically earn huge commissions. According to Pru Life's press release, the commissions earned from selling insurance range from 30 to 40 percent of the first year's premium. And amazingly, they said that their successful agents can earn as much as P2 million a year.

As with any other selling profession, you need a lot of guts and perseverance to make it big by selling insurance policies.

5. Real-Estate Brokerage

With the booming economy and property sector here in the Philippines, there's no wonder that property development projects are surfacing left and right. A real-estate broker typically earns between 3% - 5% commission on the property. If you are talking about a P3M property, that's around P100,000 commission.

Of course, finding the right buyer is close to looking for a needle in a haystack. But if you have the right network, it can be much easier.

Your Key Takeaways

Write your key takeaways or learnings from this chapter.

Chapter 3: Testing Your Business Idea and Launching It

The 1-Million-Peso Lessons I Learned after Failing 3 Times

Some businesses are inherently riskier than others. However, first-time entrepreneurs don't realize this until they have actually handled the business.

More often than not, they just look at sales and profitability as the only components for measuring the attractiveness of an idea, when there are nitty-gritties and other considerations beyond these.

Let me tell you my own story. Like most entrepreneurs, I am also the type that when I have a new business idea, I get so excited that I cannot stop thinking about it. I tell all my friends and officemates (who unfortunately don't have any experience in running a business) and they tell me they all like the idea. But then I talk to my entrepreneur friend and... boom! He tells me, *"Trust me, it's not the business you want to be in."* Point blank, he advises me not to pursue it. It's like being splashed with cold water on your face.

One minute, I am feeling so high, excitedly and passionately talking about my new-found business idea – the business that I believe will finally make me a millionaire; then, the next minute, I am falling off a cliff and hitting the ground after consulting with my entrepreneur friend. I do not understand why he is against it. To me, it seems to be the perfect business idea!

Frankly, I did not follow all of his advice. I was so passionate about my idea that I did not want to let it go. So being the stubborn person that I am, I went ahead and did it. Later on, after losing money, I found that he was right all along.

So I thought to myself, how did he know that? Is there a magic formula that I can learn? Time and again, the words of wisdom from seasoned entrepreneurs such as *"Hindi porke't marunong ka magluto, pwede ka na magtayo ng restaurant (just because you know how to cook doesn't mean you can already start a successful restaurant business)"* or *"Hindi dahil marunong ka maglaba, pwede ka na magtayo ng laundry business (just because you know how to wash clothes doesn't mean you can already start a successful laundry business),"* rang into my head.

After failing with three different businesses and talking to hundreds of entrepreneurs over the course of 15 years, I have observed a pattern with how different businesses work and what makes some businesses easier to manage than others.

I have developed a proprietary system which I call ***"Leapreneur Risk Assessment"*** or LRA. Based on my years of experience and observation, I have identified key variables that reflect the inherent risks in a particular business. It is important to note that we are talking about *"inherent risks"* here, that is, risks that are *"built-in"*. Of course, more experienced entrepreneurs can find ways to mitigate these risks and still end up very successful in that business. However, for first-time entrepreneurs, these inherent risks can make the business harder to manage.

IMPORTANT: My purpose of discussing these inherent risks is NOT to scare you or discourage you from going into business. But rather, it is to make you aware of them so you can prepare yourself better.

Now that I have made my intention clear, let's go ahead and discuss these risks. I highly encourage you to follow my system when you evaluate your business ideas and look at them in the following 3 areas:

    1.) **Financials** – are factors that affect the profitability of your business idea

    2.) **Operation Complexity** – are factors that make your business easier or harder to manage

    3.) **Long-term Viability** – are factors that make your business scalable and viable in the long-run.

Financials

1. *Does it require a huge capital investment?*

This is the first question you have to ask – as we all have limited resources, we have to make sure we utilize them effectively. As a general rule, the higher the capital investment, the riskier it is for first-time entrepreneurs. Even if you can afford it, try to find ways to minimize your capital exposure.

As I will discuss later in the chapter, I have set a personal threshold of 6 months savings as the maximum capital that I am willing to invest in a new business venture. This is because, as a first-time entrepreneur, you have to be prudent in your spending. More often than not, your first business may be your "tuition fees" for learning how to run a business. So keep it low as much as you can.

Rule: ⬆ Capital, ⬆ Risk

Quick Tips: If your business requires huge capital spending, check if you can start with the most basic equipment or product first, to lower your capitalization requirements. Remove all unnecessary add-ons at the start. If you can, outsource production/manufacturing so you can minimize capital spending. Once you become more confident with your sales, then you can increase your capitalization.

2. How is competition?

This is a little tricky because you want to avoid businesses with either no competitors, as well as those with too many. An industry with no existing competitor means that it is a new industry. While this is good because you don't have any competitors, it also means that nobody knows about your product yet. So you will have to spend more on education, marketing and building the industry.

On the contrary, industries with too much competition is not advisable because you will also have to spend more to build your own brand and become known or stand-out amidst the clutter. Some examples of these are Siomai food carts, internet cafes, ink refilling stations, etc.

Either way, you will have to spend more. So you would like to be somewhere in the middle, i.e. in an established industry with manageable number of competitors and no clear market leader yet.

If you have a revolutionary product or creating a new industry, it normally takes years to educate the market and change their behaviour. Oftentimes, first-time entrepreneurs don't have the financial resources to fund this kind of business idea.

So think twice before committing to your goal of *"changing the world."* Let the Apples, Googles, and Facebooks of the world who have deep-pockets, do the heavy-lifting. As for you, look for ideas that you can easily execute and sell fast while learning your way as an entrepreneur.

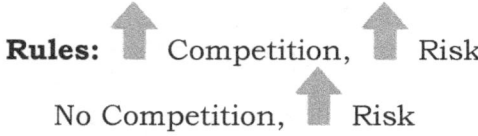

Rules: ⬆ Competition, ⬆ Risk

No Competition, ⬆ Risk

Quick Tips: Research your product well. If there's too much competition already, what you can do is to specialize in one area or niche and serve it like hell for you to standout. If there is no competition yet, talk to potential customers to gauge if there is really a problem to be solved and if they are willing to pay for it, or if it's just in your head.

3. *What's the cost-to-sales (CTS) multiplier?*

If it costs you P20 to make a product and you sell it for P100, then your cost-to-sales multiplier is 5x. That means you multiply the cost of P20 by 5 to arrive at the selling price of P100. In this transaction, you earn P80 (P100-P20) or 4x the cost.

The higher the multiplier, the better it is for your business because you are able to absorb unexpected costs and fluctuations in sales. Imagine if you have a low multiplier, say 1.5x (which means your margin is only 0.5x or 50%) and the price of your main ingredient suddenly increases by 50%, then all your profits is suddenly wiped out. Or what if your top salesperson resigns and suddenly, your revenues drops, how will you then pay for your fixed costs like rent and electricity?

We will have more discussions about fixed costs and variable costs later in this chapter.

Generally, retail businesses focusing on basic goods like rice and grocery items have a low cost-to-sales multiplier (typically less than 1.5x). Same goes with retailing of well-established products like cellphones and printers because the sheer volume of transactions can very well cover the fixed costs.

On the other hand, food and niche products and services, that typically have low volume of transactions, tend to command a higher cost-to-sales multiplier. In the food cart business, it is common to have more than a 3x multiplier. For example, siomai, which typically sells for P30 in a food cart actually costs only P5—that is a 6x multiplier!

Similarly, in the service industry, it is common to have a 3-5x multiplier.

As a final note, if you have a niche product or service, try to sell your product for at least 3x the cost to give you enough profit to recover your fixed costs like rent, as well as give you allowance for any sales fluctuations. In the real world of retailing, not every day is Christmas day so you have to make sure your fixed costs are covered even during lean days.

Rule: ⬆ CTS Multiplier, ⬇ Risk

Quick Tips: Really strive to set high a *CTS* multiplier especially if you are selling a niche product. If you do not encounter any price objection, increase the multiplier again until you encounter significant price resistance.

4. *What is the projected sales and income?*

Finally, it all boils down to the projected sales and income. Just be sure that you put in a realistic sales and income projection. Include all expenses, and factor in hidden costs like the following:

- provision for expired inventory
- provision for customer returns
- provision for pilferage
- allowance for uncollected receivables (if you have payment terms with your customers)

I have a sample template that you can use to compute your projected sales and income. Kindly let me know if you want a copy so I can email it to you.

Rule: ⬆ Projected Income, ⬇ Risk

Operation Complexity

Most first-time entrepreneurs just stop at the financials when reviewing a business idea. But in reality, there are also various operational complexities that must be considered because they can make or break the business.

There are businesses I know that are based on sound ideas but executed poorly. They were mismanaged and eventually, closed down due to the operational complexities that we will discuss in this section.

1. *What's the risk of pilferage?*

Unfortunately, the risk of pilferage is real here in the Philippines.

When your business is prone to pilferage, it's very tempting for your employees to take advantage, especially when they know that you have not set up the appropriate controls yet or when they know that you have no idea yet what the "normal" sales should be.

Some examples of businesses with high risk of pilferage or mis-declaration of sales are:

a.) Quick-service businesses like spas, barber shops, etc.

b.) Businesses with inventories that are hard to measure or count like ink refilling, restaurants, fruit shakes, etc.

c.) Businesses with inventories that is easily replaceable from other sources like groceries, clothes from Divisoria, office supplies, etc.

d.) Businesses that don't normally issue Official Receipts.

It doesn't matter if you earn 20% from every product you sell. If your employee pockets one (1) item, you need to sell 4 additional items just to pay for the cost of the lost item. This is a very real threat, no matter how well you treat your employees. I have experienced it and my fellow entrepreneurs have all experienced it, one way or another.

A friend of mine started a *lugaw* (porridge) business. He was selling unli-lugaw for P15 only. It was supposed to be a profitable business because he said that the cost of the *lugaw* was just P3.

During the first few weeks, sales were good. He was hitting his sales objective so he was very happy. After the first month, sales began to decline. When he asked his staff about it, his staff told him it was because fewer customers come in, maybe due to *"sawa na or naumay na sa lugaw (customers are sick with the porridge)."*

Since my friend was managing the business part-time and still has his full-time job, he was not in his store during weekdays to monitor all the transactions. However, the strange thing was, he noticed that every time he spent a day in the store, sales would more than double.

Weeks past and the sales continued to decline, but improve every time my friend was in the store. Later on, he found out that his staff was pocketing the sales instead of declaring them. Due to the losses and frustration, he eventually closed his lugaw business.

How can you monitor that all the sales were being properly declared and not pocketed by your employee?

Rule  Pilferage, Risk

Quick Tips:

a.) *Put proper internal control in place.*

 If there is a high risk of pilferage, try to put internal controls in place to lessen that risk. One example you've probably seen in the stores is a sign that says "If we fail to give you a receipt, your drink is on us." It's one way of making sure that sales are accounted for and reported properly.

b.) *Try to make your inventory easy to count.*

 At Ink All-You-Can, since one cartridge refill uses 10ml of ink only, it is very hard to count the actual ink that is used if the container is 100ml. So what I did was to repack the ink to 10ml sachets good for one refill. It made the inventory management much easier.

c.) *Remove too much familiarity and predictability.*
Familiarity and predictability of the process breeds the minds of unscrupulous employees. Rotate your employees to other branches every now and then. I know a company where the delivery trucks (carrying highly saleable items) don't have a fixed route every day. The drivers only know their route on the day itself to minimize planning of a modus operandi. It's a sad reality, but I can't blame the company because they had bad experiences in the past.

d.) *Perform regular but surprise audit and reconciliation.*
It is important to do surprise audit and reconciliation every now and then to make sure that everything is accounted for. You can do this full audit and reconciliation at least once a month. On top of that, you can do spot audits or reconciliation every few days for random items (not all items because it will take a lot of time). These spot audits will keep your employees on their toes always.

2. How much inventory/SKUs do you have to manage?
One of the first things you have to check when evaluating an idea is how many inventory or items you have to keep and sell.

Let's say that you are considering two (2) business ideas.

Idea #1 is to sell printed T-shirts with your own designs. You have around 100 unique designs. Total projected monthly sales is P100,000.

Idea #2 is to sell whitening soap in 5 variants. Total projected monthly sales is also P100,000 per month.

Which one will you choose assuming everything else is equal?

Obviously, it's Idea # 2, right? Your operations will be much simpler if you can get the same sales and income by just selling 5 items rather than 800 items. Wait a minute, you might ask "Where did you get the 800, it's just 100 designs."

Assuming 100 designs, you have to cater to different sizes like small, medium, large, and X-large. So your 100 items are now 400 items and that's only for men's sizes. If you also cater to women, that's a total of around 800 items.

Here are the reasons why:

a. *Inventory is tied-up capital* – If you have a lot of items to manage, you have to make sure you have enough stocks for each item. This will eat up your cash, which is the most important asset you have when you are just starting out.

b. *Additional expenses on storage and monitoring* – If you have to store the inventory in a warehouse, that's an additional expense. Also, monitoring them and doing inventory counts are necessary expenses.

c. *Higher risk of running out of stock* - Determining the right balance of inventory to keep is hard, especially if you don't have an automated system. One wrong move and you will lose sales because you ran out of stock. Imagine if you just sold one item like Siomai, it would be very easy to manage.

d. *Higher risk of pilferage and obsolescence* – If storing your inventory is not hard enough, the risk of pilferage also increases dramatically as the number of items increase. Some inventory might also become obsolete which is an additional expense for you.

Rule: ⬆ Inventory/SKUs, ⬆ Risk

Quick Tips: If you have many items, try to focus on the most saleable items first. Don't try to sell everything. As we will discuss in the following chapter, the *Pareto Principle or 80/20* states that 80% of sales comes from 20% of your products so find those 20% and focus on them first. You can introduce the other items later on.

3. *Does it need special handling/logistics?*

Does your idea need special handling/logistics? Examples of these include frozen products, fragile products, hazardous chemicals or flammable products, or simply products that are too bulky to display or carry like furniture. The smaller the product and the less sensitive it is, the better for you.

Special handling increases your product cost and limits your expansion, shipping and distribution. For example, if you have an online shop and you want to ship nationwide, you cannot do it if your products need to be refrigerated. Or if you have interested dealers in the provinces, it will be hard for them to transport your products.

During one of the events that Ink All-You-Can participated in, the ingress was supposed to be 12 midnight so that we would have a few hours to set-up the booth in time for the 8am opening. Unfortunately, the ingress was delayed due to unforeseen circumstances and my employees, along with employees of the other brands, waited outside the venue until they were allowed to enter at around 4 AM.

One of the exhibitors there was selling ice cream products. Unfortunately, their ice cream started melting because the freezer was not plugged in. As a result, they had to go back to their office, replace the ice cream that had already melted, and then go back again to the venue to set-up their booth. This is a logistics complication that I don't have to worry about with my printer inks.

Rule: ⬆ Special Handling, ⬆ Risk

Quick Tips: Find a way to reduce any special handling requirements. If the packaging is fragile, can you have it converted to plastic? If it needs to be frozen, is there a way to let it survive at room temperature?

4. *Does it spoil or have an expiration date?*

Food products are generally harder to manage because of this factor. Highly perishable products require higher level of skills and experience so that's why I don't advise this type of business for first-time entrepreneurs.

As an example, I have a friend who is a franchisee of *"Kambal Pandesal."* He said that to keep their pandesal fresh every day, they have to throw all the left-over or unsold pandesals from the day before. They cannot sell them anymore. In fact, unsold pandesals are already factored in their financials. As a result of this, his daily profits is largely influenced/determined by how many excess breads they have to throw away at night. What a waste!

On the contrary, having a product that doesn't easily spoil lessens your headache. For example, my inks can last for 3 years so I can stock up without having to worry about products expiring.

A fellow entrepreneur who is in the donuts business shared with me that they have to collect all unsold donuts the following day. This is also to keep their donuts fresh every day.

Given this, his forecasting must be very good because if they produce more than what is needed for the day, unsold items will be scrapped. On the other hand, if they produce less than the demand, they can run out of stock and lead to customer dissatisfaction, a damaged brand reputation and lost revenue.

To make things worse, they have more than 100 branches so forecasting the sales of every single store is extra difficult. Once the product is scrapped, his expenses are not only the cost of the product, but also the delivery expense to the store, the retrieval cost back to the commissary, and the disposal of those products. This is truly a very complicated business for a first-time entrepreneur.

Rule:  Perishable, Risk

5. Is it labor-intensive?

Retail and service businesses (like spas, carwash, and restaurants) are glamorous businesses because you feel proud when your friends and relatives tell you: *"I saw your store in the mall. It's very nice!"* That's why a lot of first-time entrepreneurs really consider putting up a retail business.

However, almost all retail business owners I meet say *"Sakit sa ulo ng retail (It's such a headache managing a retail business)."* I think this is because in retail, every day is a new day. You have to fight for sales and customers every single day. Another major factor is employee management. You have to deal with a lot of people with different characters, values, and attitudes. Because of this, disputes may arise.

Lastly, if you want to expand your retail business, you need to open additional stores which will require more rental payments and more people. On one hand, having more employees is good because you help more people. However, more people also mean more headaches in the long run.

Most of the time, businesses outsource their employees, <u>not because of cost-savings</u>, but to shield them from the headaches of hiring and managing employees.

In fact, based on my estimates, when you use a 3rd party manpower provider, ***you need to pay an additional 25%*** of the employee's salary because of the Agency Fee and Value-Added Tax. But again, some owners are willing to pay this premium just to lessen their employee headaches.

Rule: ⬆ People, ⬆ Risk

Quick Tips: Find a way to automate some processes to ensure consistent quality and reduce dependence on human labor. One example of this is found in the US where carwashes are done by machines and not by humans anymore.

6. *Do you have actual knowledge about the product or industry?*

What are the secrets of the trade? What makes the formula work? How come that donut is so fluffy? Knowledge about the product and the industry can make or break your business. That's why you will be in a good position if you have that knowledge, especially when you have *"trade secrets"* or a *"special recipe or formula"* that can serve as the cornerstone of your marketing and sales efforts. This is your competitive advantage that cannot be easily stolen from you.

All businesses have its own intricacies and sometimes, you'll only know it when you get there. Aside from that, competition will always come and introduce upgraded products. You have to know the product and the industry above anyone else in order to respond well.

Of course, you can always study the ins and outs of your product and industry to catch up, though it may take some time. Just hope that your competitors are complacent so you get enough leeway to catch up.

When I started Ink All-You-Can back in 2005, I initially thought that it was an easy business because installing the Continuous Ink System seemed pretty straightforward. Just to be sure, I used my product first for two (2) months so that I knew exactly how it worked before offering it to anyone. I heavily used my printer installed with the Ink All-You-Can System to print my flyers and other marketing materials.

Then, one (1) month after, my printer suddenly stopped. It was not printing or moving and just had a blinking red light. I was afraid and thought that my product damaged the printer. I then went to computer stores that sold ink and talked to their technicians. Unfortunately, as I was describing the problem, I sensed that they were clueless regarding the issue.

After much research, I discovered something that most technicians at that time did not know. It turned out that printers have an internal counter of the number of prints or inks used. When it reached a certain number, it would stop printing unless you reset the counter inside the printer.

Since most people were using original inks that time, almost no one was reaching the maximum count because inks were very expensive. In my case, I used the printer heavily because my inks were very affordable. As a result, the maximum count was reached. Thankfully, I was able to get hold of the software to reset the counter and my printer was back again. ☺

Nowadays, a lot of people know about this counter and can even reset it on their own. But ten (10) years ago, it was a trade secret that almost no one knew.

Rule: ⬆ Knowledge, ⬇ Risk

Quick Tips: Avoid industries that you have little idea about how they work. As a first-time entrepreneur, choose an industry that you are already familiar with to shorten the learning curve.

Expansion and Long-term Viability

After you've dealt with the operational complexities of your business, now you are ready to move further and think about the outlook or future of your business. If you will be quitting your job and taking the leap, it's important that your business is sustainable, stable and has a huge growth potential.

These are the next questions to ask...

1. *Is it replicable or scalable?*

What do I mean by replicable? For me, it simply means that you can expand your business by easily replicating your efforts to get the same results, like putting up a new branch or franchising your business. Scalable, on the other hand, is usually used for digital products where the business has the potential to multiply revenue with very minimal incremental cost like software downloads and eBooks.

Imagine that a business with a projected P50,000 monthly income now will be so much more attractive if you could multiply the business 10x later on. It is for this reason that franchising becomes a very attractive way of replicating your business. Think about this: if you earn P30,000 for each store but you have 100 franchisees, that easily means P3M per month! That's why it's important for you to also think about the opportunity to expand the business later on, not just the potential income now.

Some businesses, however, are harder to replicate or scale than others, especially if the business operation is heavily dependent on one person or the circumstances of the business success cannot be replicated to other areas.

I normally pass by Kalayaan Ave. when I have a meeting in Makati. Recently, I noticed that the houses in front of the PhilCare Building along Kalayaan Ave. started to set-up their own *eateries*.

I thought it was a perfect idea because the employees working in Bonifacio Global City (BGC) could eat home-cooked meals at affordable prices. With the continuous development of that area by MegaWorld, those eateries will surely have a growing captured market.

Now, if you are the *Nanay* who owns the eatery, you might earn more than enough income from the eatery to sustain your family's needs. But if you want to open up branches and expand to other areas, it will be much harder because the business scenario will be totally different, e.g. you don't have free rent, a location that's just few meters away from offices, a growing captured market, etc.

What business ideas do you think are harder to replicate?

Rule: ⬆ Scalability, ⬆ Long-term Viability

Quick Tips: Study which part of your business is replicable or scalable. For those areas that are not, try to find a way to put in a system to make them replicable or scalable.

2. *Does it have repeat business from customers?*

Entrepreneurs know that that hardest thing in business is to get customers. That's why big corporations spend a lot of money in advertising and building their brand in order to capture more customers.

Based on studies, it is 7x more expensive to sell to a new customer than to sell to an existing customer, taking into consideration all the costs involved, from advertising, promotions, personal selling, time spent explaining the product, up to setting up new accounts.

Thus, one of the quickest ways to grow your business and make it sustainable is to continue selling to existing customers. This is pretty good for service businesses like spas, barber shops and laundry shops, as well as those selling consumable products like food, water refilling stations, grocery items, and inks.

On the other hand, some products or services tend to be one-time purchases or the buying cycle is long, like houses, appliances, cars, and website development. It takes a long time for the customer to buy again from you so you have to find new customers all the time.

Selling consumables is a lucrative business, especially if the income from consumables is high. I remember in the early 2000s, mobile phone SIM cards were very expensive. They cost hundreds of pesos. However, after a few years, I think the Telcos realized that selling SIM cards was just a one-time income for them.

So now, they sell SIM cards for as low as P10.00 because they know that the profit is not in the SIM cards, but in the load (or consumables) that the customer will buy. In fact, you can even swap your SIM card from another network for free.

This underscores the fact that giving away SIM cards to hook customers to buy call/text loads can be profitable. If you think about it, when you have a Globe SIM, you are locked to buy load only from Globe, not from Smart.

What have you learned in this case? Can you offer a hook to customers so that they will buy the more profitable consumables from you?

Rule: ⬆ Repeat Business, ⬆ Long-term Viability

Quick Tips: If your product is a one-time purchase or the buying cycle is long, offer services or consumables to get repeat business from your customers.

Some examples are:
a.) If you sell a car, sell the periodic maintenance service, carwash, and lubricants.
b.) If you sell a printer, sell the inks and photo paper as well as warranty extension.
c.) If you sell website development, offer monthly maintenance and back-up services.
d.) If you are hired as a consultant to work on a project, offer a monthly retainer service after the project so they still have *"access to your expertise"* and you also have a monthly recurring income.

3. *What is the industry growth potential of the business?*

Aside from the current income, you also want to see the growth potential of the business. Are you selling a product that is in an industry that is declining (e.g. CDs, desktop computers, etc.)? Or are you in an industry that is growing year on year or about to explode, e.g. e-commerce, mobile payments, electric cars, etc.

Online Stores here in the Philippines and Taxi Apps are losing millions of pesos every month in advertising and marketing. However, they are positioning themselves in an industry that is about to explode in the next few years. When that happens, they can recover all the losses and earn huge profits.

Good for them that they have enough cash in their war chests to survive. They are prepared to lose millions of pesos until they start generating profits. As a first-time entrepreneur, you simply don't have this luxury.

Rule: ⬆ Industry Growth Potential, ⬆ Long-term Viability

Quick Tip: Avoid declining industries.

What Can You Do to Minimize Losses When Starting a Business

When starting a business, you have to take *calculated risks*. That means that you try to minimize the risk of failure by doing due diligence and taking small bets first to test your business assumptions. This is critical because as first-time entrepreneurs, your assumptions are usually way off the actual scenario. It takes years of experience to hone your *"gut feel"* about the business.

So, you must always take precautions because if you just take blind risks, you are not an entrepreneur, you're a *gambler*. This is also the reason why I'm an advocate of starting your business while still working for a company. Some people say that unless you resign, you will not be committed to make your business work. There may be some truth to that. But for me, it's better to do it one step at a time. As long as you are clear about what you really want in your life, you can make your business succeed even when you are just doing it part-time.

Here are some ways to help you minimize possible losses when starting a business.

1. **Define your Maximum Exposure and Test Period**
   It's important that before you start any business, you should define the maximum exposure that you are willing to risk for this business. You should also decide how long you want to test the business idea.

   This will keep you focused and help you avoid situations where you unknowingly spend all your money on a losing business. Here are some guidelines to help you out:

a. *6-months Savings* – I suggest that you limit your financial exposure to your first business to six (6) months of your savings. So if you are able to save P5,000 per month, then your maximum exposure should be P30,000 only for your first business.

    This is because when you are doing business for the first time, chances are high that you will lose. You are lucky if you are able to get it right the first time. At this point, you want to limit your exposure to something that is manageable. Use this time to learn as much as you can about running a business. This is real-world education that you can't get by reading books and attending seminars.

b. *24-month Test Period or Less*– In terms of giving the business time to fly, I would say within 12 months you should see signs of hope. The maximum allowance should be 24 months, unless you really have a very good reason to extend it. Otherwise, it might be time to throw in the towel and move on.

2. Focus on ONE Main Product

When you are starting out, it's easy to get so excited about the business and add different products here and there. We want to be a one-stop shop for everything. Sometimes it works out, but oftentimes, it complicates your business model and lures you away from your main product.

My advice is that as much as possible; focus on the main product first. As you become comfortable with the business, then you can evaluate if you really need to add more products or services.

3. Cash is King

Don't offer terms yet unless it's absolutely necessary. As a start-up, the most important asset you have is cash. It doesn't matter if you are profitable on paper, but if you don't have cash to pay your employees or landlord, you will quickly get in trouble. As much as possible, demand *Cash on Delivery* (COD) or better yet, an advance payment.

In addition to that, sending the invoice or bill, running after your customer and reminding him to make the payment on the due date are much harder than you think. It can be very time consuming and draining at the same time. You'd rather exert your effort on selling products than collecting receivables.

After running my business for three (3) years, all of our sales came from our retail stores in malls. We then decided it was time to get Corporate Accounts for us to expand our business. We hired Account Executives to sell our products to businesses and offer them free usage of our printer as long as they get the ink and toner supplies from us.

It was supposedly a simple idea. However, we soon realized that the corporate business is a whole different ball game than our retail business. In retail, receivables are unheard of because customers either pay in cash or credit card. But in the corporate world, most companies don't pay cash and even demand credit terms.

Thus, our receivables ballooned to the point that we had to hire an accounting person dedicated to monitoring the receivables. The logistics of sending the bills, following up for payment, and then collecting the checks was also very intimidating. It's definitely not recommended for first-time entrepreneurs, unless you have a way to make it more efficient.

4. Don't Overstock Your Initial Inventory

You might be tempted to over-stock your initial inventory to avail of a volume discount from the supplier. It's usually not a wise thing to do. Even if you have extra cash, you are better off foregoing the volume discount instead of piling up on inventory.

No matter how hard you try to project the demand for your product, as a first-time entrepreneur, your forecast will most probably be wrong. Either your estimate will be too high or too low. So it's better to stay conservative with your inventory levels.

5. Avoid Fixed Costs

Let's define some terms first. *Fixed costs* are expenses that stay the same in total amount regardless of your sales. Some examples of this include rent, salary of employees, landline, electricity, etc. On the other hand, *variable costs* are those expenses that vary significantly in total amount with the changes in sales. Some examples of this include the cost of making the product, commission or incentives, etc.

When starting your business, avoid fixed costs as much as possible because when you don't have any sales, you still have to pay for them. Thus, avoid hiring employees and renting space at the start. You should sell on the internet or sell from your home or apartment. When I was starting out, I converted my room into a warehouse where I put all my printer inks. I then sold them online and delivered the product myself to customers' homes. Even when the sales were low in the first few months, I did not have to worry about rent and salaries.

Another way to implement this is to hire commission-based sellers only. You can find people who are looking for part-time jobs who would be willing to receive a commission for every successful sale. Rather than paying them a fixed amount, pay them a commission until you become comfortable with your monthly sales.

6. Don't Pay for Expensive Ads

Use free or low-cost marketing efforts like websites, forums, and social media. Don't be tempted to pay for ads in newspapers or magazines because they are usually too broad for small businesses. Use internet marketing instead.

7. Iterate faster than the competition

If something is not working in your business, find out what it is and change it fast to see if the business improves. If you are not having enough sales, is it because of the product, the sales person, or are you talking to the wrong customer? Expect that there will be a lot of problems in the business but what separates successful entrepreneurs from others is that they analyze things and act fast before they run out of cash.

8. Monitor your financials and key metrics

Lastly, make sure that you monitor your financials like sales, inventory, expenses and profit every month. A simple Excel tracking spread sheet will do. You should also set key metrics such as the number of customers, % of new customers and repeat customers, source of new customers, etc.

Knowing these important numbers will keep you informed of your business' health and where you can focus onto take your business further.

Is Location Really Important

When starting a business, it's very important to determine the right location for you. Some companies who are not primarily in the retail business like manufacturing, accounting services, website development, video services, etc. will do well even if they are not located in a prime commercial area. However, if your business is focused on retail or services, like selling clothes, food carts, spa, or grocery, it's really important to get the best location where there is generous foot traffic or flow of potential customers. More often than not, good locations will come at a premium price.

For new entrepreneurs, it's a difficult choice. On one hand, we can *"save"* on rent by choosing an inferior location. But on the other hand, there will be less foot traffic or potential customers. One item that is often forgotten in this whole equation is the *marketing expense*. Though it's true that we can *"save"* on monthly rent, it may also mean that we have to *"spend more"* on marketing activities just to compensate for the lost foot traffic (compared to a good location). Or worse, our sales will suffer if we don't do any marketing effort.

To simplify this idea, you can find the following illustration.

GOOD LOCATION:

 FOOT TRAFFIC MARKETING EXPENSE

INFERIOR LOCATION:

 FOOT TRAFFIC   MARKETING EXPENSE

So make sure that you evaluate all the possible implications before signing the rental agreement. Check the number of people that pass by the area and make a sales projection. If you are not confident yet, take your time to gather more information first. It's very important to get a good location for your business because that can heavily influence your success. It's better to be safe than to be sorry later on.

When I was starting out, I sub-leased a small space in Shoppesville, Greenhills. That was the first branch of Ink All-You-Can with a rental fee of P12,000 per month. Sales were doing so great that I was encouraged to open another sub-leased space in Virra Mall, Greenhills.

However, I was so afraid of opening a branch in SM Malls because I learned that the rental fee were around P30,000 for a 6 sqm kiosk. That was more than double my rental fee and I thought that I might lose money.

Fortunately, a friend encouraged me to open a branch in SM just to see how it is. To my surprise, even though I paid more than twice the rental fee, my sales also more than doubled. With the same number of employees and effort in managing the branch, I earned much more because the location was simply great!

What's Next?

In the next chapter, we will discuss the Top 10 Cheap Ways to Get Your First 10 Customers. Getting your first customers is one of the most nerve-wracking experiences for a first-time entrepreneur. But once you pass it, it's one of the most liberating and confidence-building moments of your entrepreneur life.

I will also share with you my schedule when I was just starting my business and give you tips on how to manage your business part-time. It's crucial that you are able to divide your time well among your priorities in life, e.g. family, job, and business, especially during your first year in business.

I'll give you tips on how to overcome the problems that you most likely will encounter during the first year of operation, including handling customer complaints.

Your Key Takeaways

Write your key takeaways or learnings from this chapter.

Chapter 4: Managing Your Business Part-Time and for the First-Time

What are the Cheap Ways to Get Your First 10 Customers

Getting your first client is the ultimate test of your business idea. It can tell you whether you have a winning product/service or something that needs more work.

The task of getting your first client can be easier if you have done the following homework. You can easily remember it as **RISPAM**

a.) *Right Target Market* – You have identified the right target market for your product. What age, income bracket, purchasing habits, etc. You also should have a customer avatar in mind to guide your marketing efforts.

b.) *Itching Problem* – You have identified a problem that your target market is itching to solve. If it is really an itchy problem, your customers should have applied their own "crude fixes" just to suppress the itch. If they have done nothing about it, maybe it's not that "itchy."

c.) *Simple Solution* – You have the simple solution to that problem. You need to also understand what the current alternative solutions your target market is using and why your solution trumps them all. If your solution is too complicated, your customers won't bother using it.

d.) *Powerful & Clear Pitch* – You have distilled your sales pitch to clearly communicate the benefits. Observe your customers reactions and revise the pitch until you hit the bulls eye with a concise and powerful pitch.

e.) **_A_**_wesome Packaging_ – When I say packaging, it's not just the physical packaging of the product but also includes how you position your company, and how your store, website, and employees look. Make sure you have a professional logo as well as an inspiring story to tell.

f.) **_M_**_aximum Price_ – You need to understand the maximum price your target market is willing to pay. The _Clear Pitch_ and _Nice Branding_ will help you command a higher price. Raise the price higher and higher until you meet significant price resistance.

Once you have checked all the details above, you will have an easier time getting your first 10 customers. Here are some tips on where to get those critical customers.

1. Friends and Family

Your friends and family members can be a good source of customers for you. Trust is not an issue because they know you personally and will be more willing to try your product.

When you introduce your product to them, make sure that you do the whole sales pitch so that you can practice and refine it. Lastly, use this opportunity to get feedback from them as well as get their testimonials once they become happy customers.

2. Referrals

After you get your first customer and every customer thereafter, you can ask for referrals because they are an excellent source of quality leads. These referrals have been pre-qualified by your customers and at the same time, they are trusted by the people they refer. Given this, the closing rate for referrals averages between 50% - 80% because somehow you are effectively "endorsed" by the customer.

Make sure you ask for referrals from happy customers all the time. A simple question like *"Do know someone who would also benefit from our product?"* can mean huge business for you.

3. Website

The next step is to develop your own website. Given that most customers prefer searching for the product online before they make a purchase, it's a mortal sin not to have a website where you can promote your product.

A simple website that explains what the product is all about, how it works, and what benefits it can give will suffice for now. Don't forget to put testimonials on your website to make it more compelling. Lastly, you can also develop a blog to boost your efforts with content marketing later on.

You can create a mobile-friendly website for FREE in less than 10 minutes?!There's really no reason not to do it! Simply go to http://wordpress.com/and select one of their beautiful themes to get started. Once you have more money, you can convert it to a paid site later on for more options like e-commerce and more premium themes.

4. **Social Media**

This is the age of social media so don't forget your *Facebook account, Twitter, LinkedIn* and *Instagram* when searching for your first customers. I know a lot of entrepreneurs who are selling their products solely on these platforms so they really work.

Setup a Facebook page where you can post your products. Also, having a Facebook page will help you advertise your products later on.

5. **Forums/Community**

Forums related to your product are also a great way to land your first 10 customers. Just make sure that you abide by the rules of the forums to avoid being banned.

It is advisable that you join those forums way ahead of introducing your products and give helpful answers and comments so that you build goodwill in the community. That way, you can be seen as an expert in your field. You can also put your website in your signature so that people can check it out in case they are interested.

Check out the popular forums in the Philippines like www.pinoyexchange.com and www.entrepreneur.com.ph to get started. You can also search for forums specific to your target market using Google.

6. **Buy & Sell Websites**

You can post your product or service on buy & sell websites like www.olx.com.ph and bidding sites like e-bay. If you are a freelancer, you can also go to www.freelancer.com and www.upwork.com to advertise your service.

7. Tie-ups/Partnerships/Consignment

Having a partnership or tie-up with another company that serves your target market is another cheap way to get your first clients. They may already have loyal customers so piggy-backing on that is a good way to get your first clients.

When Lazada was being introduced in the Philippines, I noticed that they partnered with premier restaurants and bars in Makati by giving away Lazada P1,000 Gift Certificates. At first glance, it was something unusual because Lazada sold everything online except food.

However, a closer look at this strategy reveals that it was a perfect match. The customers in those premier restaurants and bars are the ones who have the spending power and are busy with their schedule. They are the most likely customers of ecommerce stores like Lazada and Zalora.

If you are selling food or other items, offering it for consignment to other retailers or restaurants can also help you build your business, without having to worry about paying monthly rent and managing a store.

8. Yellow Pages/On-line Directory

If you are selling products or services to businesses and you don't know which companies to approach, you can check the Yellow Pages for a complete list of companies. Search for the companies in your target industry and call them one by one to offer your products and services.

This is a very humbling experience. You need a lot of guts and patience to do this because some people might shout at you or put down the phone even before you finish your sentence. Whatever happens, just keep your cool and stay focused on your goals. We have done this and it works.

You can get the list of companies by industry and their respective addresses and contact details using online directories. Check out http://www.yellow-pages.ph/,http://www.hotfrog.ph/ and http://panpages.ph/ to get started. You can also use Google to search for more online directories.

9. Organizations

Joining organizations can be a good source of leads for your business. For example, if you are a marketing coach or targeting marketing professionals, you can join organizations like the Philippine Marketing Association (PMA). If you want to meet fellow entrepreneurs and get advice from them, you can join www.affi.com.ph. They have been helping entrepreneurs grow their business since 1997.

You can also join civic organizations like Rotary Club and Jaycees.

When I was starting my business, I joined a Rotary Club in Quezon City. During our first meeting, I met a fellow Rotarian, "Sir Ed," who expressed interest in distributing my products. Later on, he encouraged me to develop a distributorship package that we could offer to other entrepreneurs.

Through his contacts, he then helped me get my first-ever distributor, who gave meP150,000in cold cash. I remember it was my first time to hold that amount, so my hands were sweating as I carefully counted the money when we signed the deal. That deal was indeed instrumental in the history of our company because it solidified my belief that I could grow Ink All-You-Can into a full-time business.

---

10. Facebook and Google Ads

If after following the steps above you are still empty-handed or you want to boost your leads, you can try advertising on *Facebook* or with *Google Adwords*. Personally, I prefer advertising on *Facebook* because it's much cheaper and more effective for me.

You can get started with a budget as little as $10. Moreover, you can get as many as 250 clicks for that amount. You can visit this site http://www.wordstream.com/blog/ws/2014/01/30/facebook-advertising-tips for helpful tips on how to advertise on Facebook.

Note that you almost always don't have to follow the suggested bid on Facebook. Try $0.04 per click (equivalent to P2.00) first and see if you can drive traffic to your site with that budget. Just imagine, you could be able to direct 250 highly targeted people on your site with just P500.00!

Once you become comfortable with Facebook Ads, you can explore Google Ads to broaden your online advertising portfolio.

How I Managed Work and Business at the Same Time

Starting a business can be challenging since demands a lot of your time and effort. You have to research and learn all about the product, the target market, the logistics, the marketing message, and much more. Given this, time management skills are particularly important especially when you are juggling your work and your business.

In this section, I will share with you some helpful tips that helped me managed both my job and my business at the same time.

1. **Accept that you have to work harder than ever before.**
   Being a full-time employee can be stressful. Add to that the complications of starting a business and the task can be really daunting.

   However, it's not something that is impossible to do. You just have to be ready to make sacrifices and give up personal time. It's ok that you won't have much time for TV, reading or hobbies you used to enjoy as long as you work towards your goal of financial freedom.

2. **Set Specific Times for Family, Business, and Yourself.**
   It's easy to get preoccupied by the business so before you lose your way, set a specific time for your work, family, business, and yourself. Based on

experience, you only have around 20 – 30 hours to spare on your business per week, depending on how far you want to push it.

During the first few months of Ink All-You-Can, my schedule looked like below:

	Weekdays	**Saturday**	**Sunday**
Morning	Work	Business	Family
Afternoon	Work	Business	Self/Family
After Dinner	Business	Business	Rest

I usually worked on my business after dinner by researching my competitors, making my own website, doing internet marketing, making flyers and other tasks. On Saturdays, I worked on the business full-time. I then allotted Sundays for Family, Self, and God. I usually rested on Sunday evening to maintain my sanity. ☺

It was a difficult time but I really enjoyed it because I knew I was building my future back then. After two years, it finally paid off because I was able to escape the corporate world!

3. Get your family's full support.
   As you can see from my schedule above, starting a business while having a full-time job can be demanding. That's why it's very important that you get your family's support. If you have a girlfriend or boyfriend, it's a must that you get his/her full support. Otherwise, it will be a disaster because he/she will be looking for more time from you while you are busy starting your business.

Aside from figuring out how much time you should be able to spend with your family while you are starting the business, it's also important to get their help with other parts of the business. Whether it's answering the phone, counting inventory or arranging orders, giving family members the chance to help out is a great way to make them feel like they're part of your business while also getting more accomplished in less time. You can also ask a trusted family member to watch the business and reconcile sales and deposit cash while you are at work.

4. **Identify Key Metrics and Goals.**
   You need to identify Key Metrics for your business that you will constantly track to help you assess whether the business is growing or not. Aside from the usual sales and income, other important metrics that you should track include:

a.) *Total Inquiries* - Total number of people who inquired about your products or services.

b.) *Total Customers* – Total number of customers who actually bought your product or availed of your services.

c.) *Closure Rate* – Total inquiries divided by total customers. This tells you what % of those who inquired actually bought from you.

d.) *Ave. Transaction Size* – The average amount the customer pays you. Tracking this metric will help you create simple strategies for up-selling and cross-selling products.

e.) *Total Sales* – Total sales of your business. It's helpful if you can monitor this daily so you can spot any trends or fluctuations.

f.) *Total Expenses* – Total expenses of your business. Check if your expenses are within budget or not.

g.) *Total Income* – This is the amount of money left after deducting expenses from your sales.

h.) *Cash on Hand* – A very important metric to track because as I've said, it doesn't matter if you are profitable on paper. If you don't have cash to pay your suppliers and employees, you'll be in big trouble.

i.) *Cash Runway* – Total cash on hand divided by total monthly expenses. This is the number of months you can survive without any sales coming in. If this is below 3 months, you need to double your effort in getting sales.

Monitoring the key metrics above will give you an idea how your business is doing and what you can do to improve them. In fact, you can *double your profit* simply by making small improvements with your key metrics. That's what I did with Ink All-You-Can.

5. If you already have employees, ask them to report to you as often as possible.

If you have sales employees manning your cart, make sure that you ask him to report the sales by 12nn, 3pm, 6pm, and closing time via SMS. Don't ask him to report it once a day only (or worse, once a week).

Reporting sales every 3 hours or so will force him to work hard every hour so that he has something to report to you. If you ask them to report once a day only, you will not get a real picture of what hours of the day are most busy. At the same time, your employees will be tempted to take the first half of day for granted with the thinking that *"hahabol na lang sya ng benta mamaya (they can just catch up later)."*

This same strategy can be used for other employees as well. For example, you can ask them to send the number of calls for telemarketers, number of meetings for corporate sales, number of flyers given for saturation crew, or number of inquiries for a trade show.

6. Use Technology and Automate as early as Possible

With the help of smartphones, you can take care of many tasks while on the road and away from business. You can email, send instructions, or do web meetings and presentations without having to travel and endure the traffic.

In addition to this, thanks to technology, there are also affordable software solutions that you can use via monthly subscriptions for Sales and Inventory, Customer Relationship Management (CRM) and Task Management. This will enable you to use enterprise-grade software without having to buy them upfront.

Some examples are:

a.) *Email and Cloud-based File Storage* – Everyone knows Google and Yahoo. Our company actually uses GMail because of its integrations with Google Calendar, Google Drive, Google Docs and other apps.

For example, I once had a problem with my laptop's disk drive and the computer could not read it anymore. Thankfully, my files are stored in Google Drive so I was able to retrieve it using another computer. Otherwise, the documents and templates I developed over the years would have gone down the drain.

If you want to be more professional and use name@yourcompany.com email address instead of the free @gmail.com, Google actually has a business plan for Gmail, Calendar, Drive, etc. where you can use your company name. It also gives you more control on security like limiting access of company documents in Google Drive within the company only, as well as transferring access of an email to another employee in case the employee resigns.

b.) *Accounting Software* – For less than P1,500 per month, you can use online accounting software like Xero and Quickbooks Online. They have invoicing, bank reconciliation, and you can generate financial reports right away! I know a lot of SMEs who use these applications because they are pretty good for their price.

c.) *Task Management* – Assigning tasks to your employees and monitoring the progress of each task can be daunting, especially if you have more than 10 employees already. You can check out Wrike or Flow as Project Management Software to help you out. Wrike is free for up to 5 users. We use them in our company to monitor deadlines because it automatically follows up the employee to ensure that the deadline is met. That's one less thing to worry about as a business owner.

d.) *Wordprocessing and Spreadsheet* – If you want a free alternative to Microsoft Excel and Word, you can use OpenOffice. The software has improved tremendously over the years in terms of ease of use and functionality and is now pretty close to its Microsoft counterparts. If you also use Google, then you can take advantage of Google Docs where you can create documents, spreadsheets, presentations, forms, etc. online.

One cool way to use Google Docs is to create an on-line form or survey which you can send to your employees or customers via email. Then, after they submit, their answers are automatically collated for you. You can also collaborate on a document by sharing it with your employees, rather than sending it via email back and forth.

e.) *Email & Text Marketing Software* – If you like to explore email marketing, you can check out MailChimp. It's very easy-to-use and has an entrepreneur plan where you can design your email professionally and send up to 12,000 emails to 2,000 subscribers for FREE each month.

By the way, to avoid a lot of bounced emails which is a mortal sin in email marketing, you have to make sure that you have a clean list of emails by ensuring that you get the accurate email address when customers inquire from you.

Our software company, MobileOptima, developed awesome text blast and email software called *Teezly*. Using just a mobile phone or tablet, all our Ink All-You-Can branches use *Teezly* to capture the name, mobile number and email address of those who inquired from our branches. We then automatically thank them for their inquiry via SMS. Few weeks after, we send reminders in case they haven't purchased yet. We can also send them e-coupons to entice them to purchase by a certain date. The best thing is it's done automatically, without me pressing any button!

7. **Explore the possibility of having a partner in the business.**
   Although there are Pros and Cons to having a partner, you can also make it work once you have the right partner at hand. Having a partner will lessen your workload because both of you can help start the business, instead of you doing it alone.

On the other hand, I know some entrepreneurs who have been burned or cheated by their partners so be careful. Make sure that before you get into a partnership:

a.) You both have the same vision for the business, e.g. you want to just be a small local player or dominate the global market.
b.) Your partner is someone that you really trust (not just because he/she is the only one willing to do business with you).
c.) Your partner complements your skills and strengths.

It is also advisable to put everything in writing (especially the ownership and profit-sharing) as well as the roles and responsibilities for each one, to avoid any misunderstanding later on.

8. Use 80/20 Principle.

The Pareto Principle or 80/20 states that 80% of results come from 20% of your efforts. Some examples of this include 80% of your sales come from 20% of your customers, and 80% of the errors come from a few root causes. On the contrary, this also means 80% of what we do just produces merely 20% of the results.

So this simply means that the results we get are not necessarily proportionate to the efforts we put in. A few little efforts can yield significant results while other efforts can produce minimal results. So the trick is finding those little efforts that will product big results.

Given this, if you want to be more productive, you can focus your efforts on the 20% that matters and doing more of that. Since you have limited time as a full-time employee and part-time entrepreneur, you have to be certain with the things that you want to do. There is no way that you will have enough time in the day to take care of both your job and the business so prioritize those things that require little effort but produce big results.

A simple listing of all your tasks, like the one below can help:

Task	Time Required	Business Impact	Priority
1.) Revise the sales spiels	4 hours	High	Medium
2.) Call 10 potential clients	1 hour	High	High
3.) Research about a new product	8 hours	Low	Low

9. Leverage your Network.

Since you have been working in the corporate world for several years, you are lucky to have a very valuable network. Your officemates, customers, and suppliers can be an important source of leads for you. Thus, if you are looking for a supplier for your product, they might know someone that can help.

In case you also need advice on business processes like how to account for sales returns or how to put in proper controls, you can ask your company's accounting manager. Most likely, there are experts in your company that have real-world experience in the business or target market that you're in. So don't be shy to ask for their help. Request30 minutes of their time to listen and gather their insights. It's free advice that you surely don't want to miss out on! Just make sure that you tailor fit their advice to your specific business situation.

Case-In-Point

When I was starting my business, I didn't know anything about sales. I didn't know how to sell a product or how to handle a sales objection. I always told myself that I was an accountant, not a salesman. However, I quickly realized that in business, selling is inevitable. If I wanted to grow my business, I had to sell!

Luckily, I had some friends in the sales department of our company. I asked them to teach me how to do a Basic Call Procedure (BCP) and how to unmask the real objection of customers. This new skill became very handy as I grew my business.

---

10.   Use Freelancers when possible.

As an entrepreneur, you can get access to experts around the world thanks to the advent of the freelancing industry. If you are not good at designing logos, don't force yourself. Instead of spending a huge amount of time on that task, you'll be better off focusing your strength on building the business. Have it done by a professional graphics designer! Some other things that you can outsource include:

a.) Marketing Collaterals – flyers, brochures, menu, etc.
b.) Website – design and development
c.) Content Creation – articles, press releases, videos, etc.
d.) Digital Marketing – email campaigns, auto responder set-up, Google Analytics, Search Engine Optimization (SEO)

On the other hand, there are things that you need to do by yourself. This will help you understand the business further as well as protect your idea.

Some of the things that I don't recommend you to outsource include:

a.) Talking to your target market and first 50 customers
b.) Receiving the first 50 customer complaints and feedback
c.) Research and Development work

Below is the list of outsourcing sites that you can use:

a.) www.199jobs.com – Use this for simple digital jobs like article writing, logo making, transcribing audio files, etc. You can even have your own doodle video and voice-over for P199.
b.) www.raket.ph – This site has a wide range of services being offered, including business, finance, & legal, and lifestyle and entertainment. I was even surprised to see fortune tellers on their listing but I haven't tried it out yet. ☺
c.) www.upwork.com – This is an international site that has huge number of freelancers around the world. They merged with ODesk last December 2013.
d.) www.freelancer.ph – This is also an international site with huge number of freelancers. Last time I checked, they have accomplished more than 7 millions projects already.

How to Stay out of Trouble with your Work

1. Keep Doing your Job Well.

Don't let the business affect your work. Sometimes this is harder to do because we have this mentality that whether we perform or not, we will still receive the same salary. We then end up taking our job for granted.

However, bear in mind that up to this point, your work is still *your primary source of income* and you are still paid as a full-time employee, so make sure that you do your part.

2. Don't Take Advantage.

Be fair to your employer. Making calls during company hours or using your employer's supplies or equipment for your own business purposes is a big No-No. Make sure that you stay as objective and as focused as you should be during regular office hours. During weekends or after work is the perfect to focus on your business.

I heard a funny story from my entrepreneur friend of the time he caught one of his employees printing copies of their resume and application letter. The employee was apparently applying to another company. He wanted to *"save money"* so he used the company's supplies and printed the documents during office hours. *"Ang tindi nya, hindi man lang nahiya (he's such a thick-skinnned person),"* my friend complained.

When I heard the story, I laughed about it. I was guilty as well of having previously printed some personal documents using my last company's supplies. After a while, I understood where my friend was coming from. Now that we are on the other side as the employers, we know that every Peso counts so we have to take every effort in controlling our expenses. The last thing we want to see is an employee taking advantage of our resources for their own personal benefit.

---

3. Be Discreet

Don't flaunt the fact that you have a growing business on the side to your boss or officemates, or worse tell something like *"I'm earning more income from my business than what I receive as an employee."* You will be looked at in a bad light if you do that.

Disclose the real financial status of your business to your true friends only. For the rest of your officemates, just say a standard line like *"The business is doing OK but there are still a lot of things to solve."* This way, they won't make a big deal about your business until you have become really big.

4. Avoid Conflict of Interest.

Check out your company's Employee Manual to ensure that you aren't crossing any lines. Some companies have specific policies prohibiting employees from engaging in a business that competes with the company's products and services.

In case there is a conflict of interest, you may have to declare it upfront to avoid any employment issues. Better yet, start a business that does not have any conflict of interest.

5. Don't Poach Your Company's Clients

Remember that your employer is still the one putting food on your table so never bite the hand that feeds you. The last thing that you want is to get fired because of ethical issues like this. It will not only cost you your job but your reputation as well (which is very important in business). Word gets around fast so be careful.

Back in 2010, we had an employee who was very good at selling. Because of his good performance, I promoted him to be the person-in-charge of one of our big branches. Little did I know that this employee was just there to study how my business worked.

He resigned after one year and setup his own ink refilling station, together with his friends, even though it was against our company policy. What's worse is he contacted our customers and told them that we moved to a new location, which was actually his new store.

Later on, he ran into different problems so he eventually closed the business. Last year, he contacted me asking if he can come back to our company...

How to Overcome the Birth Pains of the Business

1. "Sales are not coming in."

This is probably the most common problem of entrepreneurs. You expected that as soon as you launched your business, everyone would be so excited about your product that they will fall in line just to get hold of it. Well, it rarely happens. If it happens to you, congratulations! If not, don't worry; it's not the end of the world yet. ☺

The first thing that you need to do is to find out the cause of the problem. Generally, it will fall into one or more items in the 4 Ps of Marketing:

a.) Is it because of the Product?
b.) Is it because of the Place or location of your business?
c.) Is it because of the Price?
d.) Is it because you lack Promotion? Do more people know about your product?

More often than not, if you have a good location, you can have a lot of potential customers coming your way. But if you don't have a good location, you will most probably have to spend on promotions to boost awareness of your store and product, just like what we discussed in *Chapter 3 – Is good location really important?*

On the other hand, if it is because people are not purchasing it, you have to dig deeper in trying to understand why. Is it because you failed to communicate the benefits of the product or is it because of the price?

In any case, you have to act fast to correct the problem and test if sales improve. If the sales are still not improving, you have not solved the main problem yet.

2. "My product has a defect."

One of the biggest nightmares of an entrepreneur is when he realizes that his product has a problem, e.g. not delivering the promised benefits. There is no time to waste but to find out what happened and correct it fast. Maybe the supplier sent the wrong variant of the product or maybe production was damaged.

If you have already sold the product, don't wait for the customer to discover it. Otherwise, it will severely damage your relationship with the customer. Be proactive and be the first one to inform them about the problem and offer to replace it. Your customer will appreciate your concern and honesty which is the foundation of long-term relationships with your customers.

3. "A customer complained."

Your heart might be pounding hard and fast when you receive a customer complaint. Just relax and take a deep breath. All businesses encounter this situation so there's no need to panic.

In our line of business, we normally receive customer complaints. Sometimes, they are due to normal product wear and tear. But other times, problems are caused by customer's negligence. As an example, we encountered cases where we found cockroaches and dead mice inside the printer. No wonder the printer wasn't working properly!

In any case, I tell my employees that the "Customer is the boss" so we have to properly serve them. Just ensure that you listen to the customer and do as much as you can to resolve the issue.

4. "I am short of cash."

If you encounter this problem, you have to find out why you are short of cash. It can be one of the following:

a.) *Customers are taking longer to pay* – Be careful with giving credit terms to your customers. Make every effort to collect cash on time.

b.) *Inventory is eating up your cash* – Make sure that the items you are stocking up are fast moving items. Don't stock up for the sake of getting volume discounts.

c.) *Sales are not coming in*–Kindly check our discussion in the previous section.

d.) *You've mismanaged your expenses* – Watch out for unnecessary expenses. Ask for longer credit terms with your supplier.

You might ask, *"Can't I just borrow money from the bank to supplement my cash?"* Well you can, but you have to make sure that you correct the problem first. If you are mismanaging your expenses or customers are taking longer to pay, even if you borrow money from the bank you will be short of cash again in no time.

5. "My competition copied my product."

If you competitor copied your product, it's a good sign that you are on the right track. Just think about it. No one wants to copy a bad product concept, right?

Now, you have to do some homework. Buy the product from your competitor, ask their sales staffs about it and watch how they "sell" their product to you. Which benefits are they highlighting? Are they offering your product concept first or last? What can they say about your product? Study what truly differentiates your product from the copycat and highlight those things in your *sales spiel*. Lastly, continue to improve your product so that they will not be able to catch up.

6. **"I am out of stock and cannot keep with the demand."**
This is one of the best problems to have when starting out at running a business. People just can't get enough of your products and you always run out of stocks. When you encounter this, carefully study which items are running out of stock and slowly raise your inventory level for those items. If it runs out of stock again, raise your inventory level once more. It's important to consider that sometimes demand for new products is high but over time, the excitement may wane so make sure that you don't stock too much.

7. **"My staff stole something!"**
I always believe that *"Good internal controls prevent good employees from doing bad things."* We put controls in our business to protect our employees from being tempted to do things that they will regret later on.

If you ever find yourself in this situation, assess how much was stolen. Be careful <u>not</u> to fire your employee right away because he can sue you for *"illegal dismissal."* You must collect evidence and let the employee undergo the due process before you can terminate him. While you are doing the investigation, ensure that he doesn't have access to sensitive information or valuable assets anymore to prevent further damage to your business. Consult a legal expert right away when you encounter this unfortunate situation.

A lawyer once told me about a case of a bus company that had an illegal dismissal case. What happened was that the company found out that several of their employees or conductors were not reporting the proper bus sales and were pocketing the extra cash. As soon as the company found out, they fired the employees.

Unfortunately, the employees filed an illegal dismissal case against the company because they were not given *due process*. The case dragged on for many years and when the decision came out, the bus company was asked to pay for back wages and other penalties amounting to millions of Pesos.

8. "I need to hire my first (or another) employee."

Congratulations if you feel that you need to hire your first (or another) employee. That means the business is doing well! Before you do so, try to get part-time workers first. Remember our discussion earlier that you should avoid fixed costs. As much as possible, hire freelancers or part-time workers until the demand for your product warrants for another full-time employee.

It is also helpful if you develop detailed roles and responsibilities for a person before hiring them so you can properly assess the workload and importance of the new employee.

9. "I think I need to setup my second store/branch."

Congratulations again if you feel you need to setup your second store or branch! As with the previous section, this problem requires thorough evaluation and perhaps even 10x more effort than simply hiring an employee. Setting up a second store is very expensive so you have to make sure that your business is already stable before opening another branch.

Instead of opening a second branch, you may want to consider doing home delivery, consignment to another store, sub-leasing or putting up an online store. This way, you can still reach more customers without having to put in a huge amount of capital until the time where you are confident that opening a second store is the best alternative.

10. "I'm not sure if I can do or want to do this anymore."

Being an entrepreneur is really hard. It's not a walk in the park like most people think. A lot of entrepreneurs failed several times before they made it big. If you are asking yourself whether you want to continue or not, you are not alone.

To help you out, you have to go back to the reason why you started the business in the first place. Is it because of financial freedom or flexibility? Are those reasons still important for you? Have things changed since the last time you made that commitment to be an entrepreneur?

By knowing what we really want in our life, making decisions can get easier. Know your priorities and what you want in life. If you are just afraid to fail, remember that *"You cannot taste the sweetest of sweets, if you have not tasted the sourest of sours."* Success is sweetest when you've been through tough times.

When to Throw in the Towel and Move on

A common question most first-time entrepreneurs ask is how to know when it's time to abandon the business idea. Of course, you don't want to quit too early and not give enough time for the business to mature. On the other hand, you also don't want to quit too late when you've lost too much in terms of money and time.

My answer is that you should check the results versus the *maximum capital exposure and testing period* you've set in the previous chapter and stick with it. Don't fall in love with your idea to the point that you are blinded by it. After running the business for a year or so, the numbers will objectively tell you whether there's something in it or something's not right. If it's too much of a loss, let it go and move on to your next test. Hopefully by that time, you've become smarter with running a business.

Most of us have to pay our *tuition fee* in learning how to do business. I know. I paid mine.

Your Key Takeaways

Write your key takeaways or learnings from this chapter.

Chapter 5: Taking the Leap of Faith

What Are the Five Signs That You Can Now Quit Your Job

If you have reached a point where you are beginning to consider quitting your job to go full-time with your business, congratulations! That means your business must be growing and you are starting to feel the urge to jump in with guns blazing.

For me, I worked hard on it for more than a year – working on the business every night and during weekends while focusing on my job during weekdays. Then one day, I was able to confidently say to myself that it was time to **take the leap** and become a **Certified Leapreneur**!

But that did not arrive as easy as it sounds. When I made the decision, I had to get the support of my family and friends. That time, I was travelling around the world on paid business trips, staying in five-star hotels and earning 6 figures from my job. As you can imagine, it was hard for my family and friends to understand why I wanted to leave the corporate world to concentrate on my business.

But eventually, when they realized how passionate I was with the business, when they saw how my eyes twinkled every time I had a breakthrough idea for my business, when they experienced how I couldn't help but get so excited at the chance to implement my strategies, they became very supportive of me.

So in this chapter, I will share with you the things that you need to do before you finally take the leap of faith. Let's start with the Five Signs that show you are now ready to quit your job.

1. **Your profit is equal or more than your Take Home Pay**

   First and foremost, you should make sure that your income from the business should equal your net salary plus bonuses.

   For example, your monthly salary is P50,000 and you have 2 months' worth for your bonus, that brings your total gross salary to P700,000. Deduct your applicable tax and you get your Net Annual Salary. You can divide it by 12 months to get your monthly take-home pay. You then compare it to your average business income for the past 6 months to know if you are financially ready.

   Being in business is not just about passion alone. We also have to be practical about it. More often than not, other people are relying on us, like our family, our parents, or other relatives. We need to feed ourselves, help our family, and buy the things that we need. If our income will decrease when we become a full-time entrepreneur, it's not the right time yet.

2. **Your business has been profitable for at least one year.**

   Aside from the absolute amount, you also have to make sure that it is stable and can sustain your needs for the years to come.

   It's very common for a business to have fluctuating income during the first year of operation. Sometimes sales are very good in the first few months until it hits a wall after that. Other businesses have a slow start, where they lose money in the first few months until it suddenly explodes and everyone can't get enough of it.

   That's why we have to go through the whole cycle of **at least one year of profitability** before we let go of our job. Put simply, if you are losing money during the first year and then become profitable on the second year, you have to wait for that whole year of profitability before you can resign.

I have a friend who started a *Buffalo Wings* food cart in a cafeteria in one of the buildings along Ayala Ave. During the first month, sales were phenomenal. People were curious about what the new food was all about so they wanted to try it. Sales continued to increase in the second month.

However, on the third month, sales began to decline. The same thing happened on the 5th until it stabilized by the 6th month. Unfortunately, sales at that level couldn't cover the fixed cost so he eventually closed it down.

On hindsight, there was something he overlooked. It turned out that after trying the Buffalo Wings for 3 - 5 times, it lost its appeal so they wanted to try other food. Unfortunately, there were not enough customers in the building to sustain the business considering that people would not eat Buffalo wings every day.

Good thing he did not resign from his job yet.

---

3. Business is increasing year on year (at least 30% increase)

It's not enough that the business is profitable, we also want to check if we are just scratching the surface and we can unleash its full potential if we go full-time.

Thus, the next important questions that you should ask yourself are:

a.) *"Is the business growing year on year by at least 30%?"*

b.) *"If I put in the additional effort and focus on the business, will it grow even further?"*

Think about this: if the business will not grow exponentially when you work on it full-time, you are better off just hiring a manager who can operate the business. That way you still keep your salary plus you get income from your business (minus the salary of the manager). You will still earn more with that arrangement, compared to what you get if you quit your job.

4. Cash in the bank is at least 12 months of your monthly expenses

This is easy to compute. Just look at your bank account and check whether the balance is enough to cover your monthly expenses for the next 12 months or so.

If your monthly expenses is P30,000 (include rent, food, utilities, clothing, entertainment, etc.), you should have at least P360,000 in your bank account in cold cash, *not receivables or inventory*. If you don't, wait for the cash to reach that amount before you sign that resignation letter!

You might ask, *"Why do I have to have that cash in my bank? The business is profitable anyway."* Well, it's better to be safe than sorry. You don't know when you will have emergencies like a hospitalization or sudden need for cash. As an entrepreneur, you cannot request for a cash advance or salary loan anymore. It's all up to you now. Be prepared before you jump.

5. You are ready emotionally and can't wait to leap.

If you passed the first four signs, then your business is ready for you. The last question is whether *you* are emotionally ready for your business.

When you take the leap, your world will totally change. Your work hours will change and so will your friends and officemates. Sometimes, it's lonely at the top. You don't have someone readily available to share your problems with, whether it's about your employees, your competitors, or your business in general.

The good news is that you can join entrepreneur organizations like *AFFI* to meet fellow entrepreneurs and new friends who understand what you are going through. Your world may change but it sure is an exciting world waiting for you.

What to Expect When You Quit so You Don't Get Shocked

As we've discussed in the previous section, your world will change once you take the leap of faith. It is important for you to understand what to expect so you can prepare for it.

Here are some of the things that you can expect to happen:

1. **No more employee perks.**
   Say goodbye to healthcare, bonuses, free travel, free lunch, give-aways, vacation leaves, etc. When you become an entrepreneur, you have to pay for your healthcare, travel, lunch, and everything else.

   Given this, you have to check if you need some adjustment in your lifestyle. Maybe instead of buying eating in a fancy restaurant every week, you can do it only once a month.

   TO DO: Let go of those perks and focus on building your business.

2. **No more lunch buddies.**
   Your favourite buddy cannot join you during breaks anymore. You can get physically disconnected with your officemates and friends, so you just have to content yourself with Facebook updates to know what is happening with their lives.

One thing I observed is that your lunch buddy normally serves as your stress reliever. When you have problems with your work or stressed with your boss, you have your officemates who are willing to listen to you. But once you go full-time, you will not have your peers anymore. Thus, you don't have someone readily available to listen to your problems about your business or your employees. This situation makes it extra harder to bear. That's why some people say *"It's lonely at the top."*

As I've mentioned, this also opens up opportunities for you to meet new friends and build relationships with fellow entrepreneurs.

TO DO: Meet fellow entrepreneurs and new friends.

3. It's not an 8-5 job anymore.

When I was working as an employee, I knew exactly what time I needed to wake up, what transportation to take, and how many minutes it took to get to the office. When I got there, I knew what pending items I needed to work on, what meetings to attend, and what deadlines to meet... even where to get lunch and *merienda.*

On my first day as a full-time entrepreneur, I did not know what to do. I was just at home watching television and still couldn't believe that I finally escaped the corporate world! A few days after that, the need to work sank in but I didn't know where to start. How much time should I spend doing strategic work, selling and getting clients, doing office tasks, managing my staff? Those were new things to me so I had to build my new daily routine.

TO DO: Build your new daily routine.

4. There is no regular 15-30 salary anymore.

As an employee, we are assured of a salary every 15th and 30th of the month. Whether the sales of your company go up or down, you are assured that you will receive your pay.

As entrepreneurs, we always have to save for the rainy season. Business might be good this month, but it might fall next month. As a result, our income fluctuates so make sure you budget your financials carefully.

TO DO: Budget your financials carefully.

5. No more "good job!" from your boss.

As an employee, you can easily get feedback or commendation from your boss if you do a good job. It makes you feel better and fulfilled with your job.

Now, your employees cannot say "great work!" to you because you are the big boss. If you like verbal commendation or approval to boost your morale, you need to find other ways to uplift your spirit or get it from your family and friends. Don't expect your employees to give it to you.

This might sound trivial for most people, but for some it might be a big deal. In fact, I know someone who had issues with this. After being an entrepreneur for 2 years, he said that he wasn't happy and he wanted to go back to the corporate world.

I asked him why since his business was earning and he was helping a lot of people. But then when I dug deeper, it turned out that he was longing for appreciation and verbal commendation, which unfortunately, no one was giving him.

TO DO: Assess where you get fulfilment from and do something about it.

6. No more mentor.

I was lucky to have very good bosses in P&G. Whenever I had problems or didn't know what to do, I could always ask for their advice easily.

That all changed when I became an entrepreneur. No one was there to mentor me anymore so I had to figure it out on my own. Luckily, getting business mentors are easier now. You can just join an entrepreneur organization and you'll find people who are willing to help you.

TO DO: Actively look for new mentors. Join organizations and events for entrepreneurs.

7. No more experts or assistants.

In the corporate world, when you have questions about HR, you can ask the HR manager. If you have questions on legalities, you can ask the corporate lawyer. Companies usually have multi-functional teams composed of sales, marketing, finance, legal etc. when working on a project.

As an entrepreneur, you may not have access to those experts or assistants to help you out. When you have a project, like launching a product, chances are high that you are the authority in marketing, sales, accounting, legal, etc. Don't be afraid to wear different hats and multi-task. As you grow your business, you can always hire those experts.

TO DO: Study the basics of marketing, sales, accounting, HR, legal to keep yourself abreast with the aspects of the business.

8. The buck stops with you.

When it comes to making hard decisions, having a boss comes in handy. As an employee, you don't have to make the hard decisions for the company. Also, if the decision made by the president of your company proves to be wrong, there is little chance that you will get affected, unless it leads to the downfall of the company.

As an entrepreneur, the buck stops with you. You are the one ultimately responsible for everything, including making difficult decisions like firing an employee or going for an all-out war against your competitor.

TO DO: Make sure that you are comfortable making big decisions for your company. Indecision may cost you money so you have to make a stand once and for all.

How to Get Support from your Family and Friends

Since you began your part-time business, you may have always gotten support from your family and friends. By now, you probably realized how important it is that they are fully aligned with your goals in life.

Generally, families are fine with part-time businesses, but when you talk about quitting your job, it might be a different story. Nonetheless, it's a must that you get their full support. So here are the 3 steps that I can suggest for you.

1. **Explain why you want to be an entrepreneur.**
   Help your family understand why you want to be an entrepreneur. Aside from the glory and freedom, you are most probably doing it for them anyway.

   For example, you want to be the one to bring your kids to school and fetch them in the afternoon. You want to play with them without having to worry about your deadlines and night conference calls with your boss. In short, you want to spend quality time with them later on. But for now, you have to establish the business first and make sacrifices.

   Once they realize that it is really what you want and in the end, the whole family will benefit, you'll get their "yes!"

2. **Assure them that you have done due diligence.**
   Assure your family that you have done due diligence, i.e. you have managed that business part-time, studied the different aspects of the business, and you now feel that your business is ready to fly once

you are there full-time. You can even tell them that in fact, your income from the business is already the same as your income from your job. Most importantly, tell them you plan how to even grow it further.

Most probably, your family is just really concerned about you. But once they hear that this is not a *"spur of the moment"* decision and that you have done the necessary steps to ensure that you are ready, they will be more open to the idea.

3. **Ask for their help and support.**

Lastly, as always, ask for their help and support. Tell them that it will really mean a world of difference if you get this. It's just so much easier and you will feel relieved and confident when you have their blessing.

Leapreneur

How to Say Goodbye to Your Boss & Officemates

Now that you received the blessing from your family, it's time to go ahead and tell your boss about your plans. Just make sure that you follow the appropriate lead time on resignation so you don't interrupt the operation. Most companies have a 30-day notice period so honor it. It's the least that you can do for the company that put food on your table for years and helped you get where you are now.

Here are some reminders for you:

1. **Thank them for their support.**
When you talk to your boss, sincerely thank him/her for their support and for helping you grow as a person. When you look back at the time you started with that company, you'll realize how much you've matured and grown as a professional. And honestly, you owe it to them. There are companies who let their employees become stagnant for years and you are lucky your company took good care of you.

The same goes for your officemates. You've shared lunch, laughter, and late-nights together so thank them for those experiences.

2. **Don't burn any bridges.**
In any situation in life, whether it's with your relatives, friends or officemates, it's never a wise idea to burn bridges. You entered the company properly so make sure you do the same when you exit.

Return your laptop, manuals, phones, and other company property in your possession. In case they request for one month extension on the effectivity date of your resignation to give them enough time to find a replacement, willingly oblige. Spending another month as an employee will not hurt you that much, but it will keep your relationship with your boss and company intact.

3. Tell your boss that you are interested in working on a project basis.

Tell your boss that in case the need arises, you are interested to work on a project basis. It will be a good way to keep the door open for you in case your plan didn't work out right.

When that project comes in the future, try to accommodate it if you can. It's nice to catch up with old friends and officemates when you work on that project. If you can't accommodate it, decline politely by saying that you would love to do the project but you are just so busy with very important tasks and your boss will understand.

4. Tell them that you will keep communication open.

Don't forget to tell your boss and officemates that you will keep in touch with them and they will appreciate it. They will receive an SMS or call from you from time to time just to catch up.

Also, ask them if you can call them in case you need advice about something. That will set the stage and when the time arises, you can *call a friend.*

5. Tell them to refer their friends.

Lastly, tell them that in case they know somebody who needs your product or service, you'll appreciate if they can refer them to you. Referral is a powerful way to get your customers and this is the first step in growing your business – maximizing your network.

Leapreneur

Checklist before You Resign from Your Job

CHECKLIST	DATE
☐ Business income is equal or greater than your current take-home pay.	
☐ Business has been profitable for the last twelve (12) months.	
☐ Business has increased at least 30% vs. last year.	
☐ You have cash in bank worth 12 months of your monthly expenses for emergency purposes.	
☐ You don't anticipate any huge medical expenses in the next 12 months, i.e. no baby to be born or no scheduled medical operation.	
☐ You have a clear plan to grow the business 2x. If you can't grow the business 2x by going full-time, don't resign. Just do it part-time unless you are really dying to escape the corporate world.	
☐ Check if you have an option to take a leave of absence for three (3) months before resigning. If your company allows it, don't resign yet. Just take the leave of absence first so you can *"test drive"* your plans to grow the business and experience how it feels like to be a full-time entrepreneur.	
☐ You have a back-up plan in case things don't materialize in a year's time.	

☐ Your family is aligned with and fully support your decision to go full-time.

☐ Your boss and officemates support your decision.

☐ You prayed hard and asked His guidance.

☐ Relax and take the leap of faith!

Your Key Takeaways

Write your key takeaways or learnings from this chapter.

Chapter 6: Getting Ready for a Successful Future

Is It Worth It

Being an entrepreneur is _not a walk in the park_. Being an entrepreneur will not probably give you more time during the first few years. In fact, it will suck more time from you, demanding at least 10 – 15 hours of work.

When you become an entrepreneur, you need to be ready to be a delivery person, a sales staff, an accountant, a janitor, a production staff, etc., and be prepared to do things that you will not voluntarily do as an employee. You will try, maybe fail, and then try again. So be prepared...

Some of you might ask, _"Is it really worth it?"_ Well, if you are passionate about it and it makes you happy and fulfilled as a person, then it's all worth it. As a bonus, when you hit the jackpot, you can help more people while enjoying financial rewards way much more than you can get as an employee.

For me, I've been so blessed as an entrepreneur. Let me recount the reasons why I left my 6-figure salary to be a _leapreneur._

1.) Freedom
"I felt that even though I was earning that much, I was a slave to my work."

I'm able take full control of my life. I'm no longer a slave to my work but rather, I'm now the driver of my own life. I can accelerate to 100 kph if I want to or take it slow and just enjoy the scenery. It's all up to me.

Sure, I got rid of my old boss, but the reality is, I have a _new boss_. In fact, I have many bosses now – my customers. Because even though I am the President of my company, they can fire me anytime by simply not buying from me and giving their money to my competitors instead. So when they need something, I have to make sure I deliver. But nevertheless, I can still confidently say that I'm free now.

2.) Flexibility
"I wanted to bring my kids to school and go on family vacations whenever I wanted to."

During my first few years in the business, I was really working harder than when I was employed. But right now, the organization is already in place. We have different departments already, like Human Resource, Accounting, Customer Care, Logistics, Technical, Warehouse, Production, Sales, and Audit. Each department has its own Department Head and we meet once a week to discuss the metrics.

On a day-to-day basis, the company's operation is already being handled by the department head and my General Manager. Thus, I already have the flexibility that I want. In fact, I only go to the office four (4) days a week.

3.) Financial Rewards
"I wanted to retire by age 45 without worrying about where to get our food and my kids tuition fees."

The financial rewards allow me to send my kids to the best schools, go on vacation where we want, drive my dream car, and soon, build our dream home in a nice place where we will retire in the future.

As Mark Cuban said, *"In business, it doesn't matter how many times you have failed, you only have to be right once. And then everyone can tell you how lucky you are."*

It's really comforting to know that you only have to be right once. In my case, everything I lost in my first 3 attempts in business, were all recovered (plus more) when I hit it right, with Ink All-You-Can.

4.) Passion

"I want to explore, learn new things, and follow my passion."

On top of the benefits already mentioned, I'm also lucky to work on my passion. I love developing products and introducing them to customers. Being in business challenges me as a person as well as builds my character. Because of the business, I have experience and knowledge now about marketing, technical, warehousing, sales, customer service and so much more. Things that used to make me scratch my head, I now fully understand. As result, my perspective about the business has improved drastically and became more holistic.

Besides, I was able to write this book because of my passion. Had it not been for my passion and the flexibility of being an entrepreneur, writing this book will not be possible.

5.) People

"I believed that I have the power to help at least 1 person eat 3 times a day."

Lastly, nothing can come close to the fulfillment I get when I create jobs and help other people. I have employees who thanked me because they were able to fix their house or send their kids to school or even something as little as buying new pants and shoes.

I also take pride at being able to develop people from entry-level staff to department heads and even general managers. I was able to unlock their true potential, something that they thought they never had in them. Helping other people and giving them hope and confidence in their selves is indeed priceless.

ste███████: your right sir. iba talaga ang nagagawa ng sincerity. ang saya po talaga namin sobra lalo na kung ma praise namin kayo and the management. hayaan nu po sir magsisikap po kami lagi para po sa company na nag ampon po sa akin ng kailangan ko ng masisilungan

thank you po boss the company has always been good to everyone. good bless ink all you can.

I remember when I was resigning from P&G, my co-employees asked me during my *despidida*, *"Why do you want to do it? Why do you want to forego the corporate life that you currently have, for a life as an entrepreneur which is full of risks and uncertainties?"* I said to them. *"I take pride when I see one person eating 3x a day because of my business. Even if it's just one person, it is still ONE person who can live a decent life because of me."*

Now, I am much prouder that *Ink All-You-Can* gives employment to not just 1 person, not just 10 people, but more than 100 deserving employees. Is it worth it - all the troubles and the pains that I have to go through as an entrepreneur?

You bet it is!

The Leapreneur Blueprint

We've gone through a lot of steps and details in this book. Before we finally close this book, I would like to share with you the **Blueprint** that I followed when I took the leap from employee to full-time entrepreneur.

I call this the **Leapreneur Blueprint**.

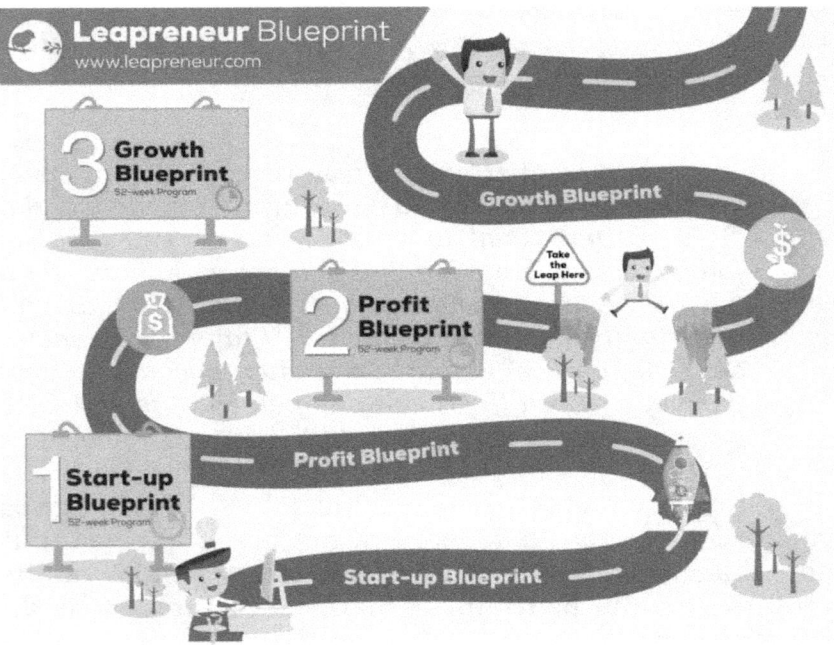

As you can see, it is divided into 3 important Phases:

Phase 1 Goal: Start your own business
Phase 2 Goal: Maximize profits from your business
Phase 3 Goal: Grow your business

Each phase in the Leapreneur Blueprint has its own goal and its own set of challenges as well.

For example, in **Phase 1 or starting a business**, you will be more concerned on finding the right product or service, pricing it right, finding the first 100 customers, creating your brand name, etc.

In **Phase 2 – Maximizing Profits**, you already know that you have a viable business and a product or service that your customers want. The challenge then becomes more on finding efficiencies or savings, converting more leads into paying customers, increasing the sales from each customers, making sure that customers come back for more, etc. to maximize your profits.

It is important to note that only after maximizing the profits from your business and meeting the criteria that we discussed in the previous chapter, you can take the leap and become full-time entrepreneur or a *Certified Leapreneur*.

In **Phase 3 – Expanding Your Business**, you have already maximized your profits from your existing branches, so the goal now is to replicate the success and open more branches or expand to other locations. The challenge then becomes putting in proper controls to ensure that everything is accounted for, documenting policies and procedures to standardize the process, implementing systems to make sure that the process is working and not too dependent on any employee, etc.

As a Certified Leapreneur, you can expand your business thoroughly. It's very hard to fully expand the business while you are still a part-time entrepreneur. Expanding a business requires time, resources, and careful analysis.

LEAPRENEUR STEP-BY-STEP PROGRAM
Many people are asking me if I have a program that will guide them *Step-by-Step* as they go through the

different Phases of the Leapreneur Blueprint. Initially, I thought that there were many seminars or trainings out there that supposedly teach people how to do it.

However, after hearing many of them tell me that there's none like it, I decided to dig dipper and find out what are the options available to aspiring entrepreneurs.

Here's what I found:
1.) There are many seminars or trainings on how to start a business but most of them do not provide actionable steps that the participants can easily follow.
2.) After attending trainings or seminars, most participants are still confused and don't know where to start. They need **simple step-by-step guide** on exactly what to do and how to do it.
3.) Most aspiring entrepreneurs NEED a nudge to start and to keep them focused on starting a business. Since they are also working, it's easy for them to delay their dream and one year after, it's still a dream, nowhere near reality.
4.) Most aspiring entrepreneurs get stuck at some point so they need someone to answer their questions to help them get unstuck. Unfortunately, seminars or trainings don't provide this important access to business mentors.
5.) There are very few trainings or seminars available for maximizing profit and growing your business. Some of the few trainings or seminars available are designed for large companies that are often not applicable to SMEs.

Given this, I decided to create my own Step-by-Step Leapreneur Program for each of the 3 Phases. At the core of these programs is what I call the **"Weekly Action System"** where each week, I will give you a specific item to work on. Unlike seminars or trainings, the system is action-oriented, with simple and easy steps to follow.

Chapter 6: Getting Ready for a Successful Future

I believe that if I can just motivate you to take just ONE action each week, you will be way ahead of other people, 6 months after. The best thing is when you get stuck somewhere, you can simply post your question and we'll be there to answer it.

If you are interested to learn more about the Leapreneur Program, just click on the link below:

www.leapreneur.com/ProgramDiscount

Enter this Coupon Code: **LPB10** upon checkout to get **10% discount** as another gift for you for purchasing this book.

How Badly Do You Want It

Congratulations! You've finally made it to the last page of this book. I hope the time and effort you spent reading this book has been worthwhile for you. As I've said, I wish there was a book like this when I was just starting out. Maybe it would have saved me hundreds of thousands of pesos in losses!

Now, I'm very happy that I had the chance to share my insights, tips and learnings with you. I believe that my mistakes in the past were not wasted since I was able to share them with people like you. It's the reason why I wrote this book. Like with my *despedida*, I feel like, *"If I can just help one person avoid the same mistakes that I did and successfully start his own business, this book will be all worth it for me."* And I do hope that you will be that person.

Before I let you go, I'd like to ask you something **_very important_**. I've seen a lot of employees who just dream about being an entrepreneur someday. They think of business ideas but never took any action. Some have tried but when they failed, they easily gave up. They want to be an entrepreneur someday but they never made that someday today.

There are a million reasons <u>not</u> to be an entrepreneur. There are also a million reasons why you should be one. I have already shown you the way and equipped you with my knowledge to help you cross it. But in the end, you are the one who will decide if you want to do it or not.

As I've said, it's not going to be a <u>*walk in the park*</u>. You might encounter failures and a lot of disappointments along the way. But one thing is for sure, when you finally succeed, it will all be worth it, just like what happened to me.

You might be afraid and don't know if you can actually do it. For me, nothing is impossible. It all boils down to this question: *"How badly do you want it?"*

If you are really <u>serious</u> about starting or growing your business, join the **Leapreneur Program** and let's make it happen!

Next Steps

1.) Download my Entrepreneur INSIGHTS as my Bonus Gift for you using this link:

http://www.leapreneur.com/FREE

Once you download it, I will also automatically enroll you to the *Leapreneur Show* where you can listen to the stories of successful entrepreneurs on how they started their business – All for FREE!

2.) Discuss the **Top 3 Key Takeaways or Learnings** that you got from this book with 2 – 3 friends and family members. Sharing those learnings with other people helps you internalize and remember your key takeaways.

3.) If you are serious about starting or growing your business, join the Leapreneur Program and we'll make it happen, step by step!

www.leapreneur.com/ProgramDiscount

Use coupon code: LBP10 upon checkout to get 10% discount.

Good luck and see you in the Entrep Community!

Your Key Takeaways

Write your key takeaways or learnings from this chapter.

www.ingramcontent.com/pod-product-compliance
Lightning Source LLC
Chambersburg PA
CBHW051914170526
45168CB00001B/378